From Sea to Shining Sea

*To Bill Diane —
Blessings!
Perry*

FROM SEA TO SHINING SEA
On U.S. 20: Boston to Newport, Oregon

All Right Reserved 2010 by
Perry Treadwell

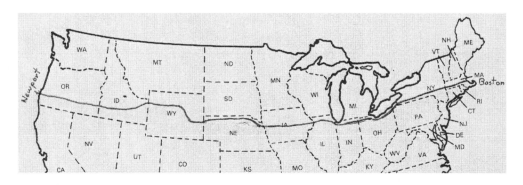

Copyright © 2010 by Perry Treadwell

All rights reserved. No part of this book may be reproduced, stored, or transmitted by any means—whether auditory, graphic, mechanical, or electronic—without written permission of both publisher and author, except in the case of brief excerpts used in critical articles and reviews. Unauthorized reproduction of any part of this work is illegal and is punishable by law.

ISBN: 978-0-557-55028-9

Previous Publications

Making Friends
Grandfather Stories
God's Judgment? Syphilis and AIDS
Last Negro In County is Dead
The Way of Friendship
Driving Through History

Dedicated to my traveling campanion, Judith Greenberg.

Introduction

Allons! Whoever you are, come travel with me!
Traveling with me, you find what never tires.
The earth never tires;
The earth is rude, silent, incomprehensible at first – Nature is rude and incomprehensible at first;
Be not discouraged – keep on – there are divine things, well envelop'd;
I swear to you there are divine things more beautiful than words can tell.
"Song of the Open Road" Walt Whitman

This has been a work in progress, a voyage of discovery of history I never learned in school or have forgotten. When I became aware that U.S. 20 was that last cross-country highway that was not an interstate, I became curious about what the road had to offer. I began this travel across the continent in Illinois. After looking at a map of the highways across the U.S., I determined that the highway through the eastern half appeared too cluttered with industry to be interesting. U.S. 20 paralleled interstate 90 presenting a concern that the surrounding land was too built-up. So I published *Driving Through History* of the western route.

Once I finished traveling the western half of the highway, I discovered the massive amount of American history that could be learned or relearned along this eastern corridor. So I started out all over again discovering, or more appropriately, putting together the history that I found so fascinating east of Chicago. Maybe this history was so intriguing this time because I didn't have to learn it for exams.

Many, many years ago I was asked by my U.S. history teacher in junior high school, "Perry, what have you heard from Commodore Perry?" My answer was, "haven't seen him recently." Then I quickly redeemed myself by adding, "We have met the enemy and they are ours; two ships, two brigs, one schooner and one sloop." My interest in history has been with me the rest of my life as can be seen by the flavor of my books. But I have become aware through the years in researching these books of the vast amount of history I never absorbed in school. And how some of it would have made that history more interesting to myself and other students.

So come with me along the U.S. 20 corridor as we follow, together, the flood of migration across a land full of wonders and perils of which novels are made. This trek is separated into two volumes and within them chapters for each state we pass through. We start in Boston where a great amount of American history began. Over three thousand miles later we reach Newport, Oregon named after its sister-city in Rhode Island, birthplace of religious freedom.

Compared to U.S. 50

Tom Brokaw has taken TV viewers on some brief stops along U.S. 50 touted as the last cross continent highway. It begins in Ocean City, Maryland on the East Coast then trough Salisbury and Cambridge to cross the Chesapeake to Anapolis. There it becomes a multilane-like interstate as it penetrates the Washington D.C. web finally breaking out in Arlington to head for Winchester, Virginia. West Virginia is next through the towns of Bridgeport and Parkersberg before heading into Ohio and the towns of Athens, Chillicothe, Hillsbero before winding through Cincinnati. Crossing into Indiana it passes through North Vernon, Seymour, Ratford, and Vincennes.before reaching Illinois and Olney. After Salem, it joins I-64. It leaves St. Louis on I-44, then heads off to Jefferson City only to get lost in Kansas City. It escapes I-470 in Kansas on to I-35, the Kansas Turnpike, leaving the pike at Emporia. The long stretch through Newton, Hutchinson, Dodge City, Garden City before Lamar Colorado. La Junta, Pueblo, Salida, Gunnison, Matritrase and Grand Junction carries it through Colorado. In Utah, it travels with I 70 over half the state before escaping to Delta and Ely, Nevada, then Carson City to Sacramento where it piggybacks on I 80 into San Francisco.

I suggest that there are many more miles on multilane highways on 50 than on 20.

VOLUME ONE

BOSTON, MASSACHUSETTS, TO CHICAGO, ILLINOIS, ON U.S. 20

A bloody land of warriors, speculators, rebels, pioneers, militia, and revolutionaries

CONTENTS

Introduction	vii
VOLUME ONE BOSTON, MASSACHUSETTS, TO CHICAGO, ILLINOIS, ON U.S. 20	1
INTRODUCTION TO VOLUME ONE	5
CHAPTER ONE: MASSACHUSETTS	13
CHAPTER TWO: NEW YORK	27
CHAPTER THREE: PENNSYLVANIA	41
CHAPTER FOUR: OHIO	49
CHAPTER FIVE: INDIANA	63
CHAPTER SIX: ILLINOIS	69
CHAPTER SEVEN: LESSER KNOWN	73
EPILOGUE	87
Sources	95

* Date Constitution ratified or statehood

INTRODUCTION TO VOLUME ONE

"The white is after Indian lands and resources. He always has been and always will be. For Indians to continue to think of their basic conflict with the white man as cultural is the height of folly. The problem is and always has been the adjustment of the legal relationship between the Indian tribes and the federal government, between the true owners of the land and the usurpers."

Deloria, Vine, Jr., *Custer Died for your Sins,* 1960, p 174 quoted in *Beyond Conquest Native Peoples and the Struggle for History in New England,* Amy E. Ouden, 2005

The history begins at the Plymouth Plantation but quickly moves to the Massachusetts Bay Colony and Boston. The way west moves along the Boston Post Road, which became U.S. 20, to Springfield. As I learned writing the previous book, the encroachment of the white colonists onto Indian lands began almost immediately. After the massacre of the Pequots (1636) at Mystic, Connecticut, and King Phillip's War (1676-77), the relations with the Indians were linked to a series of European wars between the French and British (1690-1763). The end of the Cromwellian revolution in England occurred at the Battle of Worcester in 1660 with the establishment of King Charles II. After the battle, about 8,000 prisoners were sent to New England, Bermuda and the West Indies as indentured servants.

North America has seldom been as peaceful as some would like to believe. This continent served as a pawn in the European wars for national dominance. Collectively, King William's War, Queen Anne's War (the war of Spanish Succession), King George"s War (War of the Austrian Succession) and the French and Indian War (Seven Years War) should be called the Colonial French and Indian Wars. Hardly had this series of wars ended when the sides flipped and the colonists were fighting the British with French help in the Revolution and the War of 1812. The violence on this continent gives credence to a quotation of the 17th century cited by historian Keven Phillips: "[T]he God of English-speaking Protestants was . . . a God of Warr [sic]." No wonder George Washington warned of "foreign entanglements."

Reading Steve Rajtar's *Indian War Sites* focusing on Massachusetts, New York, Pennsylvania, Ohio and Indiana presents the danger to those pioneers hardly mentioned in school history books. It took a particularly strong character to overcome the fear that must have permeated the minds of the settlers. For example, of the 34 bloody confrontations that Rajtar lists, 28 occurred during King Philip's War.

The corridor from Canada on Lakes Champagne and George to Albany was in constant turmoil as colonists fought for its control. One impression from reading these engagements might be–when will the white men start recognizing the chance of ambush? Ambush, subterfuge, trap and slaughter were common. A theme just as prominent is the slaughter or capture and enslavement of civilians.

The prevailing attitude of the white invaders was that the heathens were savages and ethnic cleansing resulted. But Native Americans used a clan, tribe and federation social structure. The Iroquois, for example, had a confederation of tribes to mitigate clan and tribe retribution centuries before the white man brought his wars to the continent. The Federation still meets near Syracuse, New York. It was a model for Benjamin Franklin's proposal of federation of the colonies during the French and Indian War.

Court documents show that the Native Americans remaining within the colonies attempted to use English law to prevent the land grab by the colonists. One example is the centuries' long court/legislative battle by the Mashpee-Wapanoag Native Americans of Cape Cod to establish their independence. Many of the Indians were "praying Indians." That is, they had accepted Christianity. That seemed to make little difference over the centuries.

The last chapter of Adams' book, *Revolutionary New England*, is titled Civil War. He states that, "In a very real sense the American revolution in one of its aspects was a civil war –- not the obvious one between the mother-country and the colonies but one between conflicting parties in each." The role of the Tories, the Loyalists, in the American Revolution is hardly mentioned in U.S. history classes.

CHRONOLOGY

WAR in North America	DATES	WAR in Europe
King Philip's	1656-57	
King William's	1690-97	War of the League of Augsburg
Queen Anne's	1702-13	War of Spanish Succession
King George's	1744-48	War of Austrian Succession
French and Indian	1755-63	Seven Years War
Pontiac's	1763-65	
Lord Dunmore's	1773-74	
Revolutionary	1776-1783	French assist Colonists
Ohio Country	1790-1795	
War of 1812	1812-1814	Napoleon against the allies

GEOLOGY

Compared to the violent geologic landscapes that I found in the far west I expected a rather benign transit in the East. I learned that the glaciers were only the last machines that modified the land. Beginning about one billion years before the present, continents and micro continents collided, separated and floated on a sea of liquid rock. The first collision, The Grenville, left the Berkshire highlands of Massachusetts. Then, half a billion years later collisions of microcontinents created what would become eastern Massachusetts. Volcanoes along the coast were responsible for the Taconic mountains. Later the land masses floated back to again collide and form the Alleghenies rising as high as the Himalayas. Millions of years of erosion whittled them down to the size one sees today. Finally, the glacier ice scrubbed the several rock formations leaving the skin of detritus on the bones of igneous, metamorphic and sedimentary rocks. Under this mantle of glacial soil is an essentially north-south stream of faults and rifts.

CONDITIONS LEADING UP TO REBELLION

> "The Americans have made a discovery that we mean to oppress them; we have made a discovery that they intend to raise a rebellion against us. We know not how to advance; they know not how to retreat." Edmund Burke, 1767 Quoted in *The Unknown American Revolution,* page 89

The conflicts leading up to the American Revolution appear, in hindsight, to be a class war between the wealthy and the yeoman farmers and tradesmen. In 1745-46, yeoman farmers twice raided the jail in Newark, New Jersey, opposing the incarceration of one of their own. The land in the first half of the 18th century was covered with large estates in obvious contrast to yeoman farms. On the large estates in the Hudson river valley, tenant uprisings occurred during th 1750s. In 1766, Chief Nimham's testimony of Native American ownership was ignored by the manor owners and the dissident tenants were evicted. This move came back to haunt the revolution when the same farmers joined the Loyalists. In the midst of this turmoil, a wave of religious renewal caused by itinerant preachers challenged the Anglican Church. This Great Awakening created a demand for equality. In Virginia as elsewhere, Baptist preachers were martyred for speaking out. In response, George Mason brought the first expressions of religious freedom to the state.

In 1770, the farmers lost another land dispute to the manor owners. Ethan Allen, quoting John Lock's observation that if you improve the land, it is yours, formed the

Green Mountain Boys. They erected a counter government judging the New York government as corrupt as King George. During the war Allen, along with Benedict Arnold, was part of the capture of Fort Ticonderoga and secured the guns that convinced the British to leave Boston.

Boston, as our school books have implied, was a hot bed of protest. Riots broke out opposing the impressment of townspeople for British naval service. This led Sam Adams to create the beginnings of a class war promoted in the *Independent Advertiser* before 1748. In 1763, the wealthy merchants took over the town meeting. The mob tore down the home of the stamp distributor Andrew Oliver in 1765. The Lieutenant governor was next. This mob violence spread to Newport, Road Island. Not only were some homes pulled down but informers were tarred and feathered. The more benign Sons of Liberty stayed out of the fracas.

A general nonimportation movement was the response to the Townshend duties in 1767. Then came the Boston Tea Party when the angered merchants sent their employees to dump the East India Company tea. This was not a tax protest but a protest by merchants not favored with the East India Company tea including Alexander Hamilton. The port of Boston was closed in retaliation. The American response was the call for a Continental Congress.

Western Massachusetts has always been at odds with the Eastern Establishment. In July 1774, Pittsfield citizens moved to shut the Berkshire County Court in anticipation of Parliament revoking the 1691 charter. Similar actions of farmers in Worcester forced mandamus counselors to resign. Then came Springfield. In many instances the number of participants was in the thousands, prescient of the French and Russian revolutions. But the fuse was lit in 1775 at Lexington and Concord and the cannon [sic] exploded July 4, 1776. As Gary Nash explains, the force of the minute men lasted not much longer than that minute and the war was fought by soldiers from the lowest classes who expected to be paid: Irish and Scotch immigrants (as were my Patton ancestors) and some Germans. Some were jailbirds as were the British soldiers they were fighting.

There was little glory and a lot more misery in the ranks particularly during the first years of the war.

The English yeoman, transplanted to this new land, brought with him the independence, propensity for mob action, and distrust for landed gentry and English courts. On the other hand, the transplanted cavaliers arrived as speculators to continue the model of British capitalism and imperialism. The spread of population across this land was based on grab and greed. The foot soldiers of this conquest being the rapidly breeding yeomanry.

CHAPTER ONE:

MASSACHUSETTS

Constitution ratified February 6, 1788

"Haveing undertaken, for ye glorie of god, and advancemente of ye Christian faith and honour of our king & countrie, a voyage to plant ye first colonie in ye Northerne parts of Virginia, . . . "
Mayflower Compact 1620
"... I have found the Massachusets [sic] Indian more full of humanity, then the Christians, and have much better quarter with them." Thomas Morton, 1632

Heading for Virginia or New York, the Pilgrims' first landfall, after a wind-blown-journey, was Cape Cod. Nearly the first day after the Pilgrims had landed, they were fighting Indians. Caught stealing cachets of corn, the starving men exchanged fire power with the Nausets' arrows.

Moving onto the area of present day Plymouth, the Pilgrims found the area had been cleared and cultivated. Only the bones of the former inhabitants, who had been decimated by an earlier plague, remained. The first winter the Pilgrims survived with the help of an English speaking former captive, Squanto. Some historians question whether the colonists could have sustained themselves if the land had truly been "virgin." Subsequently, friendly relations were established with Massesoit, the sachem (leader) of the Pokanlkets.

Counter to the popular belief that the native inhabitants lived primarily by hunting, they depended on agriculture. But the arrival of the Europeans changed the Native American culture. Trade of laboriously prepared fur pelts for European manufactured goods, such as firearms and English wool, created a cottage industry for the natives. Sir Walter Raleigh observed, that second after the "christinization" of the heathens was trade. The currency was wampum made delicately of shells by shore Indians.

Two years after the survival of Plymouth Colony, Miles Standish attempted to rescue a group of ragtag colonists in Wessagusset (present Weymouth). He enticed the Indian sachems into a meeting and massacred them. This action made it impossible for the English to stay in the area. Nevertheless, the Massachusetts Bay Colony was established in 1630.

BOSTON

The compulsive traveler can start on the waterfront at the Boston Tea Party and Museum. It is hard to imagine what it was like to sail into Boston Harbor in mid 17th century. Passing many islands, the traveler would finally view the three hills of Pembeton, Beacon and Mt. Vernon. Maybe there would be a signal fire on Beacon Hill and a drum beat to announce the arrival of a ship. Embark at the town dock at the end of King Street. Today you tie-up at Long Wharf and head up State Street to Tremont and then Beacon Street to the Common.

The traveler may begin highway 20 at the Boston Common where Quakers were hung by the Puritans for proselytizing. You may see the statue of the only woman hung, Mary Dyer, in front of the State House on Beacon Street. (See chapter 7.) Then there is the rose garden, Fenway Park and Boston University. Cambridge is just across the Charles River. In Cambridge, a young Puritan minister bequeathed his massive library and half his estate to a college to train new clergymen. The new college named the institution in his honor, Harvard.

Under the leadership of John Winthrop the basically separatist Puritans planted Calvinism from Boston along the post road to Watertown. Quakers were not the only people proscribed by the Puritans. Ann Hutchinson migrated with her large family to escape the persecution by Charles I. Unfortunately for the male leaders of the Bay Colony, she could read and held meetings where she presented her own interpretations of the Bible. At her trial (1637) in Newtown, later called Cambridge, she was banished for "false revelations."

Hutchinson traveled first to Rhode Island, then to the Bronck (Bronx) area of New Amsterdam where she was killed by Indians (1643). Her decedents, she had 14 children, include a pre revolution governor of Massachusetts as well as Franklin Roosevelt and George H. W. Bush.

Passing through **Watertown** on highway 20 is a history lesson. From April to July in 1775, the Provincial Congress of Massachusetts met in the town after leaving Concord. It became a center of revolutionary activity during the British siege of Boston. General Joseph Warren headed for Bunker Hill from Watertown. Warren, one of the primary conspirators in the rebellion, was killed in the battle. It is ironic that when the Congress failed to provide a pension for his children Benedict Arnold did.

Soon the residential homes of **Waltham** and Brandeis University come into view as Main Street becomes two lane before it crosses I-95. The Waltham Watch Company opened its factory in 1854 and is considered one of the pioneers of the Industrial Revolution making its product on an assembly line. The company lasted more than 100 years.

A number of high tech companies line I-95. Downtown, Moody Street hosts an active restaurant and nightlife atmosphere. The Charles River runs through the town offering a Riverwalk. Highlights include the Gore Place, the Lyman Estate, the Robert Treat Pain Estate, and the Charles River Museum of Industry.

The mainly two-lane street from Waltham to Marlborough flows through a nearly continuous tunnel of old trees, homes about the same age, and nodes of small business catering to the residents. In **Wayland**, highway 126 leads north to Concord and the "rude bridge."

U.S. 20 is now the Boston Post Road and passes through **Sudbury**. Sudbury contributed the most militia members during King Philip's War and also a militia to the clashes with the British at Lexington and Concord. The Wayside Inn claims to be the oldest operating inn in the country and is the subject of Henry Wadsworth Longfellow's Tales of a Wayside Inn.

The area around **Marlborough** attracted fur trader John Howe in 1656. His interactions with the local tribe of Pennacooks helped settlement a year later. The settlers protected the tribe from other Indian incursions. It became one of the "Praying Indian Towns" which was nearly destroyed by other Indians during King Philip's War in 1676. Known for its shoe manufacturing, Marlborough still has a Rockport Company outlet. I-495 cuts through the town affording access to high tech industries.

The Town of **Northborough** is typical of a New England village with picturesque churches and public buildings. Incorporated in 1766 and becoming a full-fledged town in 1775, it retains its small town flavor.

Passing through Grafton with its Hassanamessit Reservation and then Charlton, the traveler reaches **Sturbridge** south of Worchester. The highway passes mostly industrial and run down scenes possibly due to the nearness to I-395, I-90 and I-84. At times the highway rises to bucolic vistas. The highlights here are Old Sturbridge Village, the Lincoln House and Tantiusquesld Park.

Tamtiusques Park

Owned and maintained by the Massachusetts Trustees of Reservations, the Nipmuck word means "black stuff between the hills" referring to the graphite deposits. In 1644, the younger John Winthrop bought and developed the mining operation taking modest amounts of lead and iron as well as graphite. When the land was purchased from the Winthrops in 1784 it eventually became the site of the Dixon Ticonderoga pencil factory. A trail through the property affords an opportunity to walk off some of the travel miles.

Decaying vegetation pressed into peat and cooked by further pressure becomes coal. Graphite is highly metamorphosed coal.

Old Sturbridge Village

Right outside of Sturbridge rests the Old Sturbridge Village a reconstruction of a New England village of the 19th century and a must see on the trip. Take time to pay the admission and wander through the buildings moved from other parts of the country and rebuilt: a Friends (Quaker) Meeting House built in Boston in 1796 (note it has only one front door rather than the traditional two of the time), a traditional Steeple House (Quakers' designation of a church) which was built in Sturbridge in 1832, a store, a bank and the Bullard Tavern as well as representations of farming and industry. (www.osv.org)

When leaving, be sure to stop at the Country Curtains store right off U.S. 20. The business is located in the Lincoln House built in Worcester in 1836 and moved to this site. Originally it was the office of Old Sturbridge Village. Named for its first owner, Levy Lincoln Jr., it hosted Abraham Lincoln in 1848. The Worcester newspaper claimed that Lincoln was introduced to "hightone society" and enjoyed "the finest meal he had ever eaten."

Palmer is a combination of villages in the Pioneer Valley united by woolen mills along the Chicopee River. The industries first employed French and Scotts and then Polish and French Canadians.

The **Springfield** area was first explored in 1635 and was colonized a year later. First named Agawam Plantation, it was renamed Springfield for the birthplace in England of its developer, William Pynchon. There was some disagreement whether it was in Massachusetts or Connecticut. Part of the town was destroyed during King Philip's War. Pynchon came to the rescue. He established an extensive farm which he left to his son John. John, in turn, conducted the first American roundup and cattle drive on the Old Bay Path to Boston, the future turnpike.

The Springfield Armory supplied Washington's troops and became famous for its rifles.

As explained in the introduction, western Massachusetts resorted to mob rule several times. Here the insurrection continued promoted by the itinerant preacher Samuel Ely after the peace in 1781. He railed against the wealthy and the tax burden. When he was jailed in Springfield, men from the area sprang him and marched north toward Northampton. The leaders were themselves jailed, then released. Ely was jailed then released. Thus, Ely's Rebellion (1782) became a prelude to Shay's Rebellion. In August 1782, delegates from 44 Massachusetts towns presented their grievances to an aged Sam Adams representing the government.

The farmer force during Shay's Rebellion (1786-87) attempted to take the armory. The rebellion was a response to the oppressive government tactics used in collecting tax debts from farmers. The taxes were raised to pay for the American Revolution.

The rebellion began in Northampton in 1786 when farmers took over the courthouse, then they invaded Worchester followed by Great Barrington, then Springfield. Two or three farmers died and the rest fled. The dissidents ranged as far west as Stockbridge where the last skirmish of the rebellion occurred. However, the rebellion led to the first Constitutional Convention in 1787. Washington was stirred up and Jefferson wrote his famous opinion to Abigail Adams: "I like a little rebellion now and then. It is like a storm in the atmosphere." The irony is that Shay, one of the leaders, was a decorated soldier during the war who, to pay his debts, was forced to sell the sword that Lafayette had given him. The ceremonial sword was for the victory at Saratoga.

Springfield became a manufacturing city: railway passenger coaches, gasoline pumps, the Duryea first gas powered car, Indian Motorcycles, and Silver Ghosts and Phantoms of the Rolls-Royce factory. The city is also famous for the birthplace of basketball and is the home of the Basketball Hall of Fame.

Westfield appears to be a bedroom community for Springfield. The scenic route into the Berkshires begins here paralleling I-90. Highway 20 first follows the Westfield River to Chester before dipping down to follow 90 to Lee. First settled in 1660, Westfield was the westernmost settlement in the Massachusetts Colony until 1725. Nicknamed the "Whip City" due to its prominence as the center of the buggy whip industry, it also manufactured bicycles, textile machinery, and precision tools. It contains several warehouses for large corporations as well as Westfield State College. Passage of the Pure Food and Drug Act by Congress in 1906 was due in part to the movement headed by resident Louis B. Allyn.

After Westfield I-90 and 20 converge to both slice through road-cuts exposing schists and quartzite of the Goshen formation of Devonian age. Both cross the

Appalachian Trail as they climb. Here is the highest point on the highway, about 1,700 feet, before descending into the Housatonic River basin. Becket Mountain dominates the view at 2,178 feet.

The traveler can spend weeks in the Berkshires and still not exhaust the opportunities for new experiences. I-90 exits onto U.S. 20 at **Lee** toward Pittsfield and the Animagic–Museum of Animation, Special Effect and Art. The Edith Wharton Estate and Gardens, called The Mount, off Plunket St. Is next. The town of Lenox was the center of opulent homes of the very, very rich from Boston and New York City. They came to play and to show off their very, very richness to very, very rich visitors. Tanglewood, home of the music festival whose name comes from Nathaniel Hawthorne's *Tanglewood Tales* is a bit farther among several choices to visit. South of I-90, in Stockbridge, is the Norman Rockwell Museum.

Stockbridge began as a mission village for Christian Mohicans where they located their capital (Council Fire) after being forced from their traditional land in the 1740s. Their warriors served the English during the several Indian wars. The Revolutionary War split many tribes including the Mohicans between loyalty to the British or the colonists.

During the Revolutionary War, they fought in many battles but seem to be known best for what is called the Stockbridge Massacre. Around New York City, the Patriots were camped in White Plains and the British in Manhattan with forest and farms of the Bronx and Yonkers in between. On August 31, 1778, a force of Stockbridgers (as they were called) and Patriots was overwhelmed by a larger British force including the Torrey band of Green Jacked Rogers Rangers made famous during the French and Indian War. Many of the Indians were chased and slaughtered and finally buried in what is now known as Van Cortland Park in the Indian Field. From the descriptions written by both sides it was hardly a massacre. A local marker was erected in 1906.

Pittsfield itself is a pleasant town which identifies itself as the real originator of baseball. The claim is based on a 1791 Pittsfield law prohibiting anyone from playing "baseball" within 80 yards of the new meeting house. Apparently a few windows had already been broken. The Berkshire Museum right on the main street, South Street, will soon complete an addition featuring the history of the area.

The French and Indian War kept settlement away until 1752 when pioneers from Westfield arrived. The town is named after British Prime Minister William Pitt. Water power from the Housatonic River and its tributaries brought in milling. Merino sheep introduced from Spain prompted a woolen industry that lasted almost a century. General Electric had its origins in the town. Its former site is now a Superfund site due to the presence of polychlorinated biphenyls (PCBs). The $250 million cleanup continues.

While touring through New England in 1902, President Theodore Roosevelt was nearly killed--one of his Secret Service agents was--when the wagon in which he was riding collided with a Pittsfield trolley.

Today, Pittsfield is worth a stay for an opportunity to visit history in the area such as The Colonial Theatre, the Lichtenstein Center for the Arts, as well as several eating and drinking establishments.

The last stop before New York State is the **Hancock Shaker Village** a historic but still working farm of 20 buildings. The traveler should plan to spend at least three hours wandering over the farm viewing the living, eating, and manufacturing buildings as well as the gardens-- particularly the medicinal garden--the sheep, cows, pigs and horses. The visit was particularly inspiring for this former farm boy of the 1930s and 40s.

A little bit more about the Shakers. Often, Shakers are confused with Quakers (The Religious Society of Friends) from which the spiritual leader of the Shakers came: Ann Lee of Manchester, England. Since they practiced celibacy, they grew from conversion of others and adoption of children. Established in 1774, they waxed into an estimated 4,500 in nineteen major communities then waned to nonexistence. The Hancock Shaker Village was reduced to three members by 1959 and was sold to a not-for-profit corporation to preserve this National Historic Landmark.

Between Shaker Village and Lebanon Springs, New York, 20 cuts through the Taconic Range formed during the Ordovician era.

The Indian Wars are evidence of the deterioration of Native American-colonist relations.

The Pequot War

By 1636, a vibrant community was established in the Massachusetts Bay with designs on the Connecticut Valley as well as Maine. The Dutch also saw the valley for the taking. Upon the death of the Pequot grand sachem, they incited the Naragansetts to attack the English,

Using the pretext of the killing of Captain John Stone, actually a pirate kidnaping Indians for ransom, the bay colonists attacked the Pequots. This was two years after Stone's death. The Massachusetts/Connecticut area was flooded with English settlements including a fort on the mouth of the Connecticut River where it enters Long Island Sound.

A more immediate reason for war was the execution of Captain John Oldam for some act against the Narragansetts. John Endecott was sent to destroy the natives on Block Island for all the booty the invaders could recover. The foray was unproductive. The band was just as unsuccessful at the Connecticut River. Roger Williams from the colony in Rhode Island kept the Narragansetts from joining the Pequots.

In retaliation for their treatment, the Pequots attacked at Wethersfield killing six men, three women and taking two girls prisoner. With massacre in mind, soldiers and Naragansetts attacked Mystic, Connecticut, killing 300 to 700 men, women and children. Pequots rushing from Sassecus's fort nearby to help were defeated. This ended the First Puritan War as Francis Jennings calls it. Jennings, in *The Invasion of America*, considers Europe at the time much more violent than New England Indians. Indian warfare was well regulated: no burning villages, no crop destruction, no torture. War was in retaliation and regulated. The Europeans taught them "total warfare."

King Philip's War

"You know our fathers had plenty of deer and skins, our plains were full of deer, as also our woods, and of turkeys, and our coves full of fish and fowl. But these English having gotten our land, they with scythes cut down the grass, and with axes fell the trees; their cows and horses eat the grass, and their hogs spoil our clam banks, and we shall all be starved." Miantonomi to the Montauks in 1642. *Mayflower* p 179

The friendly relations established with Massesoit, the sachem of the Pokanlkets, lasted through the first generation of Pilgrims. The author of *Mayflower* judges the situation: "But as was becoming increasingly apparent, the children of the Pilgrims had very short memories. Now that their daily lives no longer involved an arduous and terrifying struggles for survival, they had begun to take the Indians for granted." He goes on to explain, "In what is the great and terrible irony of the coming conflict–King Philip's War–by choosing to pursue economic prosperity at the expense of the Indians, the English put at risk everything their mothers and fathers had striven so heroically to create. By pushing the Pokanokets until they had no choice but to push back, the colonists were unintentionally preparing the way for a return to the old, horrifying days of death and despair."

It began with the arrogance of two leaders, Philip, the son of Massesoit, and Governor Josiah Winslow. Philip acquired his "kingship" by saying that he was equal to Charles II King of England and would be treated thus. Several times he backed down when confronted with the pushy English, but, when three Pokanokets were falsely condemned for murder and hung, Philip lost control of his warriors. On June 20, 1676, the killing began in Swansea. In response, combined forces from Plymouth Colony and Massachusetts Colony headed for the Pokanoket village in present day Bristol County, Rhode Island. They found that it had been hastily abandoned.

The attitude of the English in the area, according to Phillbrick, changed to a racial war, that is, King Charles against the Native Americans. The conflict widened and Philip lost most of his tribe and any control he had over the Indians. The soldiers from Massachusetts intimidated the Narragansetts into hostility. The militia could not differentiate between friendly and enemy Indians. Many were killed or shipped to Cadiz, Spain as slaves. The "Christian Indians" were rounded up and interned on Deer Island in Boston Harbor to die of cold and starvation.

The list of lethal incidents grew over the next year: Menon, 20 miles west of Boston, Middleborough, Dartmouth, Brookfield, Lancaster, South Deerfield, Northfield. The entrance of the Mohawks on the side or the English turned the conflict and, finally, starvation ended the war. Philip was run down and killed. The remaining Indians surrendered. Some were executed. Others, about one thousand of them, were sent as slaves to the Caribbean and Africa.

Phillbrick estimates that "Plymouth Colony lost close to 8 percent of its men." He goes on to observe that, "Of a total Native population of approximately 20,000, at least 2000 had been killed in battle or died of their injuries; 3,000 had died of sickness and starvation . . . Overall, the Native American population of southern New England had sustained a loss of somewhere between 60 and 80 percent." He observes that this "local squabble" mutated into a region wide war that wiped out the Indian population much like the plague of 1616-1619.

Nevertheless, the war, instead of removing the threat of Indian attack had alienated once friends and left the frontier open to attack. "Over the course of the following century, New England was ravaged by a series of Indian wars." This forced the colonists to beg for protection from England ending the autonomy they came to establish.

The remaining Indian Wars were, for the most part, extensions of European conflicts primarily between France and England. The traveler will revisit these conflicts in subsequent chapters.

CHAPTER TWO:
NEW YORK

Constitution ratified July 26, 1788

"All the great masterful races have been fighting races . . . No triumph of peace is quite so great as the supreme triumphs of war. Diplomacy is utterly useless when there is no force behind it . . . It is through strife, or the readiness for strife, that a nation must win greatness." Theodore Roosevelt quoted by Richard Kluger in *Seizing Destiny* p564

The geology of New York state is, at first, dominated by the glaciation of the North American continent that began about two million years before the present and ended, as humans spread around the world, only 6000 years ago. The Wisconsin glaciation was at its height about 20,000 years before the present and its effects are seen in all but the southwestern edge of the state. Nevertheless, the glaciation did its work on bedrock much older. Triassic volcanoes on what is now the eastern seaboard and tectonic collisions shaped the underlining rock.

Moving from the Massachusetts Berkshires through the Taconic Mountains that make up part of the boarder, the highway drops down into the Hudson River Valley. The valley itself was gauged out by the glacier. From the Albany plain, U.S. 20 climbs past the Helderberg scarp (a sloping rise) providing good views of the route I-90 takes along the Mohawk River Valley.

The highway parallels the edge of the Allegheny Plateau on what is sometimes called the Cherry Valley Turnpike. The traveler is now on a slow developing roller coaster ride up and down troughs, at times cutting through limestone, at times through drumlins.

> (Side Bar) This traveler likes to call drumlins glacier tears. They are north-south mounds that look like human burial hills seen elsewhere throughout the world. Instead, they are of glacier construction made up of large and small stones pressed into these long, thin hummocks pointing in the direction of the retreating glacier.

Before reaching Springfield there is an overlook of the Mohawk Valley worth investigation. Farther on, after several ups and downs, the traveler reaches **Cazenova** and the opportunity to visit Chittenargo Falls as it eats away through the limestone scarp. Crossing Butternut Trough right before **La Fayette**, the traveler can watch hang gliders taking off to swoop along the valley.

Most geologically interesting, between La Fayette and Buffalo, are the finger lakes. As the glacier moved south, it gauged these north-south fingers with the resulting till (deposits of rocks of various sizes). Then, the glaciers receded leaving the till as a dam on the lake. Although the Allegheny Plateau is tilted south, the water collected in the finger lakes must run north. To get some perspective on these fingers: Lake Geneva is the deepest at 633 feet, but the bottom is filled half again with glacier deposit. At the head of Lake Cayuga lies the Montezuma Marshes. Highway 20 passes through this wildlife refuge. From **Darien Center** it is all downhill to Buffalo and Lake Erie. Of course, the must-see geologic feature is Niagra Falls.

From east to west, the route passes through the Six Nations of the Iroquois: Mohawk, Oneida, Tuscarora, Onondaga, Cayuga and Seneca. These tribes were next, after the Algonquins, to destroyed by white expansion greased by speculators and rum. It continued the clash of cultures between a subsistence way of life and dominance of land and accumulation of wealth.

Immediately across the New York state line, more remnants of the Shaker period can be found in **New Lebanon**. By 1864 the colony had more than six hundred members. In 1965, Mount Lebanon Shaker Village was designated as a National Historic Landmark. The remaining buildings comprise a Sufi retreat center and a Shaker Museum. The buildings are located right off 20 with a left turn onto Darrow Road and a right turn onto Shaker Road. If you reach the intersection with state road 22 you have passed it but can turn onto 22 then Darrow Road.

Passing into the Hudson Valley, we stopped for lunch in **Schodack** at a very popular dinner called My Place. One of the diners said that the area had been devoted to farming but was now a satellite for Albany. Continuing on what is now called the Columbia Turnpike, the towns of Nassau, East Green Bush and finally Rensselaer, are also bedroom communities for Albany and Troy. U.S. 20 crosses the Hudson River here and the highway passes through downtown **Albany**, past the capital buildings and stately residential neighborhoods before Duanesburg, Carlisle and the suburbs of Schenectady.

Battle of Saratoga

Just a few miles north of Albany, up U.S. 4 along the Hudson is the site of one of the determining battles of the Revolutionary War. Here in the fall of 1777, the British plan to take Albany and end the rebellion was blocked. The three threats to Albany were to come down the Lake Champlain/Lake George corridor, down the Mohawk River, and up the Hudson. The forts along the lakes, including Ticonderoga had been taken back by the British. The battles of Oriskny and Fort Stanwix ended the British strike down the Mohawk River.

Bergoyne's army crossed the Hudson above Saratoga Springs following many delays which allowed the Patriots to coalesce their forces including those of General Benedict Arnold. A British faint at Vermont was stopped at Bennington on August 14. One historian reports that all the Tories captured at that battle were executed.

The main battle occurred September 19 at Freeman's Farm. The British were repulsed with heavy losses. American sharpshooters picked off the officers and artillerymen. The British retreated and went into defense hoping the other two prongs would relieve them. They, however, had turned around. On October 7, the patriots attacked and again the British retreated. Bergoyne hoped to get back to Lake Champlain but the way back was blocked. Bergoyne surrendered and all soldiers and wives were sent for shipment out of the colonies. There is a monument to Arnold's leg at the site of the first battle. It recognizes his importance in the battle before his treason.

The Erie Canal The importance of the Erie Canal in the nation's expansion westward cannot be overstated. Called "Clinton's Big Ditch" for the New York Governor, it was begun in 1817 and completed in 1825. At the conclusion of the Revolution, Washington took a long ride through New York and concluded that a canal linking the Hudson River with the Great Lakes was needed. The 363-mile waterway went from the Hudson River at Troy in a wide loop to Buffalo using 83 locks to raise it to the level of Lake Erie. It helped the development of Schenectady, Utica, Rome,

Syracuse, and Rochester as well as making Buffalo a port city. Immigrants landing in New York City could travel on water all the way to Chicago. As noted in *Driving through History*, it brought goods and soldiers as well as people to the Midwest.

(Side Bar) On a spring day in the 1990s, William Least Heat-Moon, author of the book that started me on highway exploration, *Blue Highways*, set out from the Atlantic Ocean to boat across the nation to the Pacific Ocean. In his case, it was New York City to Astoria, Oregon. After motoring up the Hudson River, he entered the Erie Canal at Troy. The reconstructed canal uses more of the Mohawk River passing Herkmer, Utica and Rome paralleling I-90. Rather than traveling the short distance from Oneida Lake to Lake Ontario, the canal takes a left turn, and the long route to Buffalo and Lake Erie sometimes on the Seneca River, Cross Lake, and the Montezuma Marsh. Along the way I-90 separates the canal from U.S. 20. The canal reaches the Niagra River at Tonawanda where the river and then the lake winds and sea beat up the boat and the crew so badly they took an early portage to U.S. 20 and then south to Lake Chautauqua. They would not see highway 20 again until Souix City, Iowa.

The canal was a political as well as a construction phenomenon over apparently insurmountable odds. Building it trained the first cohort of engineers who would build America. I recommend the web site www.eriecanal.org for the traveler to explore all the tourist opportunities along the route. For example, there is a 36-mile stretch preserved at the Old Erie Canal State Park running from Dewitt, near Syracuse, to Rome.

A side trip up state road 30A north to Johnstown brings the traveler to the home of Sir William Johnston. He and his sons were significant in the mitigation of hostilities between the Iroquois and the British. He was the sponsor of Joseph Brant and Brants sister who were both significant in the last French and Indian War and the American Revolution which soon followed. The so called "half-breed" brother and sister were highly educated and acted as mediators and translators. They took the British side during the Revolution. The glue that held the shaky frontier together dissolved with the death of the elder Johnston. (See Cherry Valley below). The Mohawks headed for Canada and the Oneida allied with the Patriots.

(Side Bar) Drums Along the Mohawk, the film, 1939

In 1776, a young couple, played by Henry Fonda and Claudette Colbert, head out from Albany to homestead in the Mohawk Valley. Indians destroy their home and they struggle on. The next year an invasion force of Tories, Canadians and Indians starts down the Mohawk River as part of the British plan to capture Albany. They besiege Fort Stanwix (also known as Fort Schuler) near Rome. The poorly trained militia (as shown in the film), from Tryon County and Fort Dayton, under the command of Nicholas Herkimer rushed to relieve the fort and were ambushed by some of the force besieging Fort Stanwix at the Battle of Oriskany. It was a disaster for the militia but, drawing away the besiegers, allowed the defenders to sally out to destroy the Tory camp. The invading army turned around and headed back to Canada unable to support Burgoyne.

Fort Dayton was besieged itself by Butler's Rangers and Bryant's Volunteers (see chapter seven), but a nine mile run by an ambushed scout warned the inhabitants of German Flats. They rushed to the fort to watch their homes burn. Neither Fort Dayton nor Fort Herkimer across the river were taken. A short trip up state road 28 from highway 20 leads to Herkamer and Little Falls historic sites and state road 5 on to Oriskany. (This is a classic John Ford film based on the book by the same title.)

Similar to parts of Route 20 in Massachusetts, the road passes through run-down areas and verdant countryside, abandoned tourist cabins and farms and quaint towns such as **Carlisle.**

Just a few miles south on state road 80 lies the National Baseball Hall of Fame in Cooperstown.

Farther on is the Petrified Creatures Museum near **Richfield Springs**. Actually, the Triceratops and other monsters are a concrete introduction to the Cardiff Giant hoax.

(Side Sar) Soon after Carlisle, the traveler can take an exit off the four-lane divided highway onto state road 163 to **Cherry Valley** the site of the worst massacre during the Revolution. Tory Walter Butler, the son of John, was convicted of treason and condemned to die in 1777. Gen. Benedict Arnold gave him a reprieve but his prison conditions were as bad as Ethan Allen's (chapter 7). Gen. Lafayette had him transferred to the home of a Tory sympathizer who helped his escape. Planning revenge, he joined with Brant's Senecas also seeking revenge for destruction of their towns. They targeted Cherry Valley.

The soldiers and residents were ill prepared for an attack in the midst of a snow storm in 1778. The fort stood but the Indians could not be restrained from slaughter and burning. Fourteen soldiers and 32 inhabitants, mostly women and children, were killed and more were taken prisoner. Brant let many of the prisoners go asking that the Patriots exchange them for his wife and child to join him in Canada.

Butler, not Brant, was the villain at the massacre allowing the wanton killing. He was killed by an Oneida Indian in 1781 escaping from the Battle of Johnstown, New York, the last major battle of the war.

There is a museum in town and a monument on Alden Street to the 32 residents who died. In the neighborhood, there are walking trails as well as a beautiful falls where Hugh Mitchell is said to have hidden after finding his wife and girls killed. An interesting footnote: During World War One, filmmaker, Robert Goldstein, was thrown into jail for making a silent film containing the massacre and depicting the British (our allies) in an unfavorable light. (from slate.msn.com)

Nelson was set off from Cazenovia on the 13th of March, 1807, and received its name in honor of Lord Nelson, the great English admiral. Its population has fluctuated around 1000 for many years as a center of farming and dairy industry.

The village of **Cazenovia** is worth a stop to view the Lorenzo State Historic Site overlooking Cazenovia Lake, the Bruster Inn, a former summer home of John D. Rockefeller's partner, and Chittenango Falls.

The present U.S. 20 was built in 1934 connecting Cazenovia with Skaneateles. The highway runs through **Pompey** which was Iroquois land and then the former Central New York Military Tract. This land was used to compensate soldiers of the American Revolution. The major east-west Native American trail ran north of the present highway which became the Genesse Road in 1794 and then the Seneca Turnpike in 1800.

Once U.S. 20 passes under I-81 it reaches **Cardiff** and the site of the famous stone giant hoax. George Hull, a cigar manufacturer, wanted to spoof the Genesis reference to "giants in the earth." He commissioned a stone statue carved and had it buried on a friend's farm near Cardiff. It did create quite a stir for a while when it was unearthed.

(Side Bar)Utopia: a failed dream

Just past Madison and Bouckville, the traveler can take a 12 mile side trip up state road 46 to Oneida and the home of the former Oneida Community. John Humphry Noyes started this utopian community of about 300 people in1848. The Mansion House built in the 1860s has eight guest rooms and a museum. The members of the cult called themselves Bible Communists holding that their religion called for belief in new ideas including open sexual relationships in which all the men of the community were married to all the women. An attempt at eugenics caused enough animosity for Noyes to be indited. He fled to Canada.

The remaining members paired up. Eventually some left; a few remain. The Mansion House and grounds are worth the trip.

Now 20 enters the beautiful finger lakes region. The quaint town of **Skaneateles** lies at the head if Skaneateles Lake and a site for summer tourism. Similarly, **Auburn** sits at the head of Cayuga Lake. For 21 years Auburn was the site of Auburn Theological Seminary which moved to New York City to become the Union Theological Seminary. The Willard Memorial Chapel, the only unaltered Tiffany chapel, is located on Nelson Street. It is the only remaining building from the seminary.

This area became disputed territory after the Revolution with many Indians surrounding Fort Niagra. The British retained forts and control until the Jay Treaty or 1794 with England followed by the 1795 Treaty of Greenville dictated by Anthony Wayne. The Seneca were next to have their land contracted by speculators which the weak local and national governments could not control.

Another highlight of this trek on 20 is a stop at the Women's Rights National Historical Park right on the highway in **Seneca Falls**. Park in the rear and spend time viewing the history of the Women's Movement. The statues of these revolutionary women and men are central to the lobby and appear as they might have stood during the Women's Rights Convention. Next door is the remains of Wesleyan Chapel where the "Declaration of Sentiments" was read July 1848.

(Side Bar) The Golden Book

At Canandaigua, the traveler can take another side trip of 25 miles north up state road 21 to Hill Cumorah in Palmyra and to Mormon history. The history of Joseph Smith is told in his homes. Here the angel Moroni told Smith where to dig up the gold plates of the Book of Mormon. A pageant explaining the history is presented every July. According to Mormon history the family of Lehi sailed to America from Palestine in 600 BCE and eventually became the Indians.

After the Revolutionary War, water mills sprang up along the Seneca River which drains both Cayuga and Seneca Lakes. The canalization of the river for navigation began in 1818 allowing commerce to the Erie Canal and Lake Ontario. Canalization was completed in 1915. The rapids no longer exist.

Geneva was the site of a British fort during the French and Indian War and was destroyed during the Revolutionary War. At the head of Seneca Lake, the town served first as an industrial center and now it is a tourist attraction.

After **Canandaigua** at the lake of the same name, travelers can choose to take alternate 20 bypassing the suburbs of Buffalo. The alternate passes through farm country before **Geneseo**. This was the site of a major Seneca village. During the Revolutionary War the village was destroyed by Revolutionary soldiers because they had linked with the British. Native Americans fled to Fort Niagara where many starved to death.

By 1797, the site was being settled and the town was incorporated in 1832. The town was designated a National Historic Landmark in 1991 and has been described as "picturesque." It served as a Union training camp during the Civil War and a prisoner-of-war camp for Italian solders during WWII. The town is a center of an active farming community and serves as a bedroom community for Rochester.

Among several homes on a walking tour of **Warsaw** is the Gates house built in 1824. The Museum of the Warsaw Historical Society is its present resident. The town was also the site of strong Abolition and women's suffrage movements.

In **East Auora**, the Auora Historical Society maintains the home of former President of the United States Millard Fillmore. There is also the Roycroft Inn (a National Landmark) available for dining and accommodations. East Aurora is also the home of Fisher-Price, the toy manufacturer. Every August there is a Toyfest Festival with a parade of giant Fisher-Price toys and an amusement park for the children to play with some of the smaller toys. The Toy Town Museum contains toys from the early 1900's to today.

Now a suburb of Buffalo, **Orchard Park** was settled by Quakers around 1803. Crossing I-90, U.S. 20 heads south paralleling Lake Erie. **Fredonia** has an early history of Native American Mound Builders, then the Eries, then the Iroquois and Senecas. At this point, this traveler got on I-90 and headed for Pennsylvania and Erie.

European Wars extended to the colonies

After a brief hiatus following King Philip's War, a series of battles and treaties continued the struggle for control of the North American continent and for power in Europe. All of the treaties were signed in Europe with little or no New England involvement. In the Northwest Territories, the wars involved the French verses the British and both countries' Indian allies. It is helpful to understand the range of the Indian lands before the warfare began in 1690 to the end of the American Revolution.

From the Hudson river, the Mohican territory extended westerly toward the Catskill Mountains, northerly to the two great inland lakes of Lake George and Lake Champlain, easterly to the Green Mountains of Vermont and extending southeasterly to the Connecticut River. Their homeland encompassed present-day eastern New York and the western sections of Vermont, Massachusetts and Connecticut. Their population prior to the introduction of Old World diseases and European alcohol is estimated from between 8,000 and 25,000 individuals.

The Iraquoi land ranged west from the Mohican land into Ohio Country (see below)

King William's War 1690-1697

Both France and Briton had designs on the St. Lawrence seaway and the Mississippi water shed. On the continent, the French were fighting the English to replace

Protestants William and Mary. They had replaced Catholic James II who had fled to France. So it was also a religious War.

The governor of Canada, Frontenac, sent down raiding parties. The first group fooled the inhabitants in Dover, New Hampshire, into allowing Indian women to stay in a home over night. The women opened the gates allowing the warriors in to kill and capture the townspeople and burn the town, July 1689. This incursion began the raids. The next raid was at was Pemaquid, Maine.

Then a group of French, Sault and Algonquian Indians from Montreal found that no one was guarding the stockade at Schenectady, New York. The party was sent in retaliation for the Iroquois raids carried out with English weapons and supplies against French siding Indians. The party of about 200 French and Indians attacked at midnight on February 8, 1690 in bitter cold burning homes and slaughtering men women and children. Beside the 60 dead, 27 were taken captive most of them to Canada. The raiding party had intended to attack Fort Orange where present day Albany stands but Schenectady was a target of opportunity. The frontier war fizzled out with the Treaty of Ryswick.

Queen Anne's War 1702-1713

On the European continent, the French were still trying to establish a Catholic king in England, this time the son of James II. At the same time, the French were trying to establish a ruler of their choice in Spain. So the conflict became the War of the Spanish Succession. Queen Anne was Mary's sister who ascended the English throne after the death of William.

Just before dawn on February 29, 1704, a French and Indian force attacked the settlement at Deerfield, Massachusetts. Twenty-two men, nine women and twenty-five children were killed. One hundred and nine men, women and children who survived the attack were forced to march 300 miles to Quebec. About a fifth died on the way, 60 were eventually ransomed and some chose to remain. A replica of the village stands today for visitors to wander through.

A treaty in Ultrecht produced a lull in the conflicts on both continents. But the treaty did not prevent the French from attempting to establish their claim to the land bordering the Great Lakes and land west of the Alleghenies. This was disputed by both the English and the Indians. Beginning in 1698, French expeditions explored the Mississippi River and established a colony on Biloxi Bay and then New Orleans in 1718. By mid century, the French had more than 60 forts along the Great Lakes and down the Mississippi River.

King George's War 1744-1748

This war is also known as the War of the Austrian Succession in Europe. In North America, it was highlighted by the capture of Louisburg on a point of land on Cape Breton Island. The fort commanded the entrance to the Saint Lawrence River. A force of New England farmers and fishermen was successful in taking Louisburg.

France and England tried to put their claimants on the Austrian throne. The peace, as arranged at Aix-la-Chapelle, restored to each power what it had possessed before the war and that meant that Louisburg must be restored to the French. To the New Englanders who considered the capture a great victory, this was a slap in the face and good reason to eventually do their own governing and not depend on rule across the waters.

The French still had control of the Ohio part of the Northwest territories and much of the Mississippi Valley. We will save this history for the travels through Ohio.

CHAPTER THREE:

PENNSYLVANIA

Constitution ratified December 12, 1787

"BUT because the Happiness of Mankind depends so much upon the Enjoying of Liberty of their Consciences as aforesaid, I do hereby solemnly declare, promise and grant, for me, my Heirs and Assigns, That the First Article of this Charter relating to Liberty of Conscience, and every Part and Clause therein, according to the true Intent and Meaning thereof, shall be kept and remain, without any Alteration, inviolably for ever." Pennsylvania Charter of Privileges, 28 October 1701 by Wm. Penn

It is less than 50 miles from the New York-Pennsylvania boarder traveling highway 20 to the Pennsylvania-Ohio boarder. This highway has been called the Ulysses S. Grant

Highway and the Buffalo Road. Parts of the Great Lakes Circle Tour, which surrounds the lakes, includes highway 20. From Buffalo, New York, state road 5 parallels both I-90 and U.S. 20 through Erie Pennsylvania to Ohio where it merges with 20. Then it takes off again on Ohio 531 through Ashtabula back to 20 through Cleveland where it finds Ohio 6 through Sandusky to Toledo.

As highway 20 follows along the Lake Erie shore, it actually crosses the edge of two larger Ice Age lakes formed by the retreating glacier. The largest was Lake Warren followed by Lake Whittlesey before the present shoreline of Lake Erie appeared. The force of the ice can be understood by the dimensions of the lake today. The gouge of this first of the Great Lakes to appear is 240 miles long and 30 to 60 miles wide. It is made up of three basins: from Buffalo to Erie, from Erie to Cedar Point, Ohio, and the last one to Toledo.

Sand along the shoreline moves from west to east constantly changing the lake edge. It tends to silt up the Presque Isle harbor. Commodore Perry had to drag his ships over the sand spit into the lake using empty tanks as floats called camels.

Erie

Erie is derived from the Iroquois tribe, "the Eriez" or "Erielhonan" who lived along the lake. Presque Isle is a peninsula creating a natural harbor for the present city of Erie. The French built a fort on the peninsula in 1753 as a step in their encroachment into the Ohio Valley. The turn of the tide of the French and Indian War gave the British possession of the land where they built their own fort. Following the Revolutionary War, Pennsylvania acquired the land in 1792 as the Erie Triangle. General Anthony Wayne, whom we will meet in Ohio, built another fort there where he is buried. Eventually, the town of Presque Isle was renamed Erie and became a city in 1851.

On the "island" itself, there is much to do in the realm of recreation. There is also the Tom Ridge Environmental Center. The research center is dedicated to study the flora and fauna of the area. It has a "Discovery Center" for young students to try hands-on exhibits. The 65,000 square foot building is described as "green" incorporating present day environmental technology.

Presque Isle State Park is a wonderful site to relax and enjoy fishing, boating and swimming or just examining the light house (from a distance since it is privately owned) and the Perry Monument and Exhibit. There are miles of sandy beaches to enjoy. It is an easy jaunt off route 20 or the Pennsylvania Turnpike.

The town of Erie itself is one of the rust belt towns experiencing the transition between heavy industry and lighter commerce and tourism. There is a story about the transition of the town as a railroad hub with tracks of three different gauges coming in. This required the use of laborers to transfer the cargo from one set of cars to another. When the standardization of gauges was required, the mayor led a mob of citizens to burn the bridges and tear up the track in protest to losing their jobs.

This road along Lake Erie takes the traveler past some of the history of the French and Indian war and the war of 1812.

French and Indian War

Early in 1753 a French force from Quebec established a Fort on Presque Isle. The invaders of Indian territory then moved south to establish Fort Le Boeuf on French Creek near the present town of Waterford. This gave the company the opportunity to travel by water to the Allegheny River at Franklin and on to the junction of the Allegheny, the Monongahela and the Ohio. Fearing this encroachment into lands believed part of the Virginia land grant, Lieutenant Governor Robert Dinwiddle sent a 22-year-old George Washington all the way to Fort Le Boeuf to tell the French to get out of English territory. The French commander graciously refused. Washington straggled back.

The next year, Washington was sent back with an army of militia. Reconnoitering with a small band including some Indians, he came across a small, sleeping French force and killed many. Washington could not prevent the Indians from mutilating the dead. The French sent a large force from Fort Duquesne which overwhelmed Washington's rag tag militia at Fort Necessity in southern Pennsylvania.

The whole boarder between the French and English, nominally Indian land, was the site of French reprisals. As the French and British sent soldiers to North America, confrontation on the high seas occurred. Thus, the French and Indian War on the North American Continent became The Seven Years War on the European continent in contrast to the earlier conflicts that began in Europe. In the Spring of 1756, England and France finally declared war on one another. One historian calls this the first world war since it eventually included the Caribbean as well as Asia.

Washington was not through with Pennsylvania after his defeat at Fort Necessity. The British sent Major General Edward Braddock to confront the French in 1755. His plans were to capture Fort Duquesne, Fort Niagara, Crown Point in New York and Acadia in what was then Massachusetts Colony (Maine and New Brunswick, Canada, now). Washington joined Braddock on his arduous trek toward the Monongahela and Fort Duquesne.

As the British mass of men, canon and baggage approached, the French commander realized that he could not defend a siege. He decided to lay a trap for the bunched troops with his force of added Indians. In the clash of men, the French flanked the column. Chaos pushed the whole British army back losing most of their arms and baggage which well supplied the desperate French and their Indian allies. Washington was learning how to defeat the British arms.

The British attempt from Albany to approach Fort Niagra also sputtered to failure. The campaign up Lake George to Lake Champlain nearly ended in another ambush and disaster. Only the capture of Acadia with the expulsion of the Acadians (described in Longfellow's poem Evangeline) was successful.

Then next year, 1756, any successes of the previous year were washed away with the capture of the forts near present day Rome, New York, and Fort Oswego. The confrontations were brutal. The French turned over prisoners to the Indians to extract information and for torture. Fort William Henry at the south end of Lake George was laid to siege. When the British surrendered, the Indians attacked the unprotected civilians and troops as James Fenimore Cooper depicted in *The Last of the Mohicans*.

The war did not turn in British favor until 1758 when the French abandoned Fort Duquesne. The next year Quebec was besieged and Forts Niagra and Ticonderoga taken. It would appear that the French and Indian War had ended with the fall of Quebec and Montréal.

Nevertheless, the world war went on in other areas. Spain declared war on England in 1762 and the British captured Cuba and Manilla. The Peace of Paris (1763) gave them back. Britain took all of Canada and the land to the Mississippi River retaining the land west of the Alleghenies for the Indians. The colonists believed this land was available to them and encroachment began.

To pay for the large debt that the Seven Years War had accrued, the British started taxing the colonies with no consultation with the Americans. A dozen years after the peace treaty the British would be fighting Washington and some of the colonists.

But the trek along Lake Erie is not quite over. As will be expanded later, the end of Pontiac's War (1763-64) came with General John Bradstreet's campaign around the lake in 1764 pacifying the Indians along the way to Fort Sandusky and Detroit. (See Ohio)

The American Revolution

As we have seen in the previous chapters, most of the conflict during this so called civil war between the Patriots (aided by the French) and the Loyalists and British occurred farther east and south. Nevertheless, there was fighting and massacres in Pennsylvania and farther west.

Tory and Indian raiding parties set out to wipe out the settlers and militia. **The Wyoming Valley** followed the Susquehanna River. Near the present day Wilkes-Barre, a small fort protected the settlers. In July, 1778, a force of British soldiers, under the command of Colonel John Butler, and Cayuga and Seneca Indians, led by Cornplanter, overwhelmed the Patriot defenders. The Loyalists and Indians began killing and torturing the prisoners and noncombatants. Butler reported that 227 scalps had been taken but many more settlers in the area were killed.

When the Patriots throughout the colonies heard of the Wyoming massacre, they were outraged. Such brutality brought retribution which included George Rogers Clark's expedition into Ohio as we will see later. A Scottish poet, Thomas Campbell, wrote a poem about the atrocities in 1809: *Gertrude of Wyoming*. Thus, the state of Wyoming got its name from the poem.

Butler's son, Captain Walter Butler, led a similar force in **Cherry Valley**, New York, five months later with a similar massacre of the garrison's defenders and prisoners (described above). These two massacres moved Washington to send the Sullivan expedition do destroy more than 40 Iroquois villages in central and western New York.

Before we pass on to Ohio, the history of the **Underground Railroad** must be highlighted.

> "The Underground Railroad's impact on the antebellum United States was profound. Apart from sporadic slave rebellions, only the underground Railroad physically resisted the repressive laws that held slaves in bondage. The nation's first great movement of civil disobedience since the American Revolution, it engaged thousands of citizens in the active subversion of federal law and the prevailing mores

of their communities, and for the first time asserted the principle of personal, active responsibility for others' human rights. By provoking fear and anger in the South, and prompting the enactment of draconian legislation that eroded the rights of white (author's emphasis) Americans, the Underground Railroad was a direct contributing cause of the Civil War." Fergus M. Bordewick, Bound for Canaan, p 5-6, 2005

One cannot travel along the Lake Erie shore without recognizing the history of the Underground Railroad. From Buffalo to Detroit, small and large ports became the terminus of the great web of trails leading to freedom.

While Pennsylvania, particularly Philadelphia, was the center of the eastern web, Ohio and Indiana became the center of the western exodus. This migration actually began in North Carolina in 1780 when the Quakers decided that they could no longer have any part in slavery. The first exodus was actually Quakers who were driven out of North Carolina by angry slave holders. At what is now Cincinnati, they crossed the Ohio River to Ohio and Indiana which had been declared free of slavery. By a chance incident involving a free man kidnaped in Delaware and brought to North Carolina, they discovered the need to assist slaves to escape and conduct them north.

The river became the Jordan for thousands of slaves conducted by people of many religious faiths both white and black. By 1850, the river of slaves that began as a trickle from North Carolina in the early 1800s became a raging torrent. River towns such as Ripley Ohio and Madison, Indiana, hid the escapees from the slave catchers and opposing townspeople. Slowly but inexorably the contraband was passed along a complex and changing web of trails to Toledo, Lorain, Cleveland, Ashtabula and Sandusky where ships were found for the last leg to freedom. At Sandusky, the sailing ship, ironically named *Mayflower,* headed for Amherstburg, Canada. At times during the winter, sleighs crossed a frozen lake to Pelee Island, Canada.

The escape to freedom was always long, grueling and dangerous for the conductors as well as the escapees. Bolstered by fugitive slave laws and rewards, the routes were always through hostile territory particularly along the boarders with the southern slave states. During the half century before the Civil War it was a quiet revolution compared to the nosier abolitionist movement.

CHAPTER FOUR:
OHIO

Statehood February 19, 1803

"[N]ot even a Chinese wall, unless guarded by a million soldiers, could prevent the settlement of lands on Ohio and its dependences." (1773) Quoted by Gary Nash in *The Unknown American Revolution* page 128

Crossing into Ohio, the traveler can take a scenic side-trip on state road 534 from **Conneaut** through Ashtabula to Geneva before rejoining highway 20. There are several sites on the National Historic Register along the way including the Harbor Light at Conneaut, the harbor district in **Ashtabula** and another lighthouse at Geneva On The Lake. Ashtabula County is known for its many covered bridges and wineries. The traveler must leave 20 on state road 7 north in Conneaut to find 534. But the side-trip is worth seeing the light house and beach.

As the traveler experienced in Pennsylvania, highways 20 and I-90 travel along Lake Erie together. The traveler may not realize that highway 20 rides on the banks of the lakes that shrank to the size of Lake Erie. There are several named lakes in this history. For example, 20 follows the edge of Lake Warren near Conneaut that existed 12,000 years before the present. After Cleveland it rides on Lake Whittlesey's (13,000 ypb) beach ridge and again between Norwalk and Monroeville. Near Sylvania it crosses Lake Arkena's (13,600 ybp) shoreline. At Fayette, 20 follows Lake Maumee's (14,000 ybp) border contours.

From this description the traveler can see the effect of the Wisconsin Glaciation. When not on old lake shores, 20 crosses moraine deposits. It takes a little more investigation to find the sandstone quarries, caverns, and earlier manifestations of Ohio's geologic history. Mark J. Camp's *Roadside Geology of Ohio* is highly recommended for further study.

One can't help but pass through **Cleveland**. There is no way around it. The downtown area was laid out by General Moses Cleaveland. It was incorporated in 1814 but soon dropped the first *a* in the name, as the story goes, to fit a newspaper masthead. The swampy land along the Cuyahogo River did not deter rapid growth after the completion of the Erie Canal. The river served as a link with the Ohio River. The Rock and Roll Hall of Fame sits on the lake front.

Once the traveler passes through Cleveland, one can take a short side trip from highway 20 through the sweet college town of Oberlin. Oberlin's Down Town Historic District is only one of the many sites on the historic register which includes the college itself.

Norwalk is at the center of a subregion in Ohio's Western Reserve commonly known as the Firelands. The subregion's name recalls the founding of the area as one for settlers from cities in Connecticut that were burned during the Revolutionary War. On July 11, 1779, Norwalk, Connecticut was burned by the Tories under Governor William Tryon.

Several locations in the Firelands area were named in honor of those cities (e.g., Greenwich, Groton, New London, Norwalk, Norwich, Ridgefield) as well as the names of settlers (e.g., Clarksfield, Perkins, Sherman).

On May 30, 1800, the United States ceded the land titles to the "fire sufferers" and the representatives of the Western Reserve transferred the political jurisdiction to the general government. The Indian title was extinguished by treaty on July 4, 1805, on payment of $18,916.67. In 1806, thirteen men arrived to make the first survey of the Firelands.

On November 9, 1808, a group of prominent citizens from Ridgefield, Norwalk, New Haven, Greenwich, and Fairfield met at the courthouse in New Haven, Connecticut, as the Board of Directors of the Proprietors of the half million acres of land lying south of Lake Erie, called the "Sufferers Land." They passed a resolution naming many of the townships in this area known as the "Firelands of Ohio." By 1810, Ohio had nearly as many residents as Connecticut

The War of 1812 stalled emigration into the area. By 1819 Norwalk had a population of 109. The population grew sufficiently to be incorporated as a city in 1881.

Norwalk also has the reputation of having a virus that causes "stomach flu" named after it, norovirus, because it was the site of the first recognized outbreak of the disease in 1968.

(Side Bar) The region is known for the American legend of **Johnny Appleseed**, John Chapman, son of a nursery man, headed west in 1792 into Pennsylvania. He acquired apple seed there from cider presses and distributed them in the new farms in the Mohican area just opened up in Ohio. Although located in an area in north central Ohio, he wandered as an itinerant preacher as far as Illinois. His seedlings at various farms earned him money on shares. He died around 1845 and is celebrated, in story and song, for his simple lifestyle and love of animals.

The population of **Bellevue** was 8,193 at the 2000 census. It is part of the Sandusky metropolitan statistical area. During the first half of the 20th century, it was a busy railroad hub of the Nickel Plate Railroad, and it remains today as a hub for the Norfolk Southern Railroad.

Bellevue was the home of Henry Morrison Flagler when he partnered up with John D. Rockefeller to start Standard Oil. Flagler later went on to build the Florida Overseas Railroad, to Key West, Florida. The property of this former Bellevue residence on Southwest Street is the current location of the Mad River and Nickel Plate Railroad Museum.

Before Bellevue it might be worth taking a side trip up state route 4 to **Sandusky** and the Cedar Point amusement park which features the world's second tallest and second fastest roller coaster, Top Thrill Dragster, as well as a historic carousel on the midway. The park advertises itself as having more rides than Disney World. A lighthouse also adds to the scene.

The British established a fort in about 1794 in this Seneca land. After the Revolutionary War, the area was part of the "Firelands." Sandusky was established as the town of Portland in 1816 but soon changed its name.

Harriet Beacher Stowe wrote about the town as an Underground Railroad stop in *Uncle Tom's Cabin*. Boats took the escapees to Amherstburg, Ontario. As a footnote to history, the first Worshipful Master of the Sandusky Masonic Lodge laid out the street grid to resemble a symbol of Freemasonry. Today a large number of historic sites are found in the vicinity. Many are private homes or businesses but some appear more unique such as the Boecking side-paddlewheel at the Jackson Street Dock or the B & O Railroad Company Depot (1900).

The islands off Sandusky Harbor contain a civil war prison as well as the Perry's Victory and International Peace Memorial.

The population **of Clyde** was 6,064 at the 2000 census. The town is known for having served as the setting for Sherwood Anderson's 1919 collection of short stories:

Winesburg, Ohio. It is also the site of the Major General James B. McPherson House (1825). Born in 1828, McPherson experienced a proud military career including taking part in fortifying Alcatraz Island before being killed at the Battle of Atlanta.

Fremont's population was 17,375 at the 2000 census. It is the county seat of Sandusky County. Highway 20 goes straight through town where the Rutherford B Hays House (1850), home of the 19th president of the United States, is found.

Toledo

As the traveler approaches the Toledo suburbs through Perrysburg, a statue of Commodore Perry himself forces the traffic to turn left and cross the bridge into **Maumee**. Here a great bog existed, called the Great Black Swamp, that ran all the way to New Haven, Indiana. Mastodon bones were found nearby. State Monuments to Fort Megs and Fort Miamis are also nearby.

The area was first settled by European Americans in 1794, after the Battle of Fallen Timbers, with the founding of Fort Industry. The War of 1812 caused many settlers to flee the area. Resettled around 1817, a Cincinnati syndicate purchased a 974-acre tract at the mouth of Swan Creek and named it Port Lawrence. The syndicate failed three years later and the settlement joined with a river settlement to the north called Vistula. The inhabitants of this joined settlement chose the name Toledo.

During the construction of the state constitution it became clear that the politicians did not want slavery, conforming to the Northwest Ordinance, or the presence of Blacks. This racism would become more apparent in Indiana.

The Toledo War (1835-36) was not a war at all but a boarder dispute between the state of Ohio and Michigan Territory. U.S. 20 runs through the disputed Toledo Strip. Both militias stood up to each other and shooting could have begun. Michiganders invaded Toledo and prosecutions were carried out. President Andrew Jackson resolved the issue in favor of Ohio and its Democratic votes. In turn, Michigan acquired the land that looks like a stocking cap on top of Wisconsin and was allowed to become a state.

Toledo is known as the Glass City because of its long history of innovation in all aspects of the glass industry: windows, bottles, windshields, construction materials, and glass art, of which the Toledo Museum of Art has a large collection. Several large glass companies have their origins there. Toledo has also been known as "The Auto Parts Capital of the World." Several large, Fortune 500 automotive-related companies had their headquarters in Toledo. However, most of these companies as well as the auto manufacturing plants have disappeared.

Toledo boasts a large list of homes, churches and businesses on the National Register of Historic Sites.

The remaining route of highway 20 in Ohio passes through verdant farming country.

West of **Lime City** 20/23 hits I-475 and goes around Toledo to the south to exit west of the city on Central Ave. Where 23 continues north on 475, 20 exits west to **Assumption** and its Basilica, then **Oakshade**. This is farming country with its small towns and large farms. **Fayette** in Fulton County had a population of 1,340 at the 2000 census. **Alvordton** in Williams County had a population of 305. At **Columbia,** 20 crosses 80/90 and the Indiana boarder.

Before the traveler leaves Ohio it is worth taking a moment to sample the conflicts that influenced its settlement and development. The Ohio Valley was Shawnee and Algonquin country.

Pontiac's War 1763-65

The French had made inroads into Ohio Country in1747 attempting to wrest the alliance with the British away. Another expedition in 1752, punished the Miami tribe at Pickevillany, Ohio, for not following the orders of the previous expedition.

Toward the end of the French and Indian War the British imposed a boundary between the settlers and the Indian tribes with the eastern limits at the Appalachians and the western limits at the Mississippi. This was the Indian Reserve. Soon, General Jeffrey Amherst, hero in the French and Indian War, cut off giving gifts and gunpowder to the Indians of Ohio Country, *pays d'en haut* (upper country). A festering situation developed. The colonists depended on English soldiers for protection unwilling to contribute money or militia. The Delaware Indian prophet Neolin preached opposition to the British.

Pontiac, an Ottawa chief, riled up a sufficient number of conspirators in May 1763, to lay siege to Detroit killing everyone, civilian and soldier, outside the fort. The Indians attacked a relief column outside the fort at the Battle of Bloody Run. Pontiac abandoned the siege the end of October.

During the siege, Forts Sandusky, St Joseph, Miami (present day Fort Wayne), Ouiatenon (La Fayette, Indiana), Michilimakinac, Venanago (Franklen County, Pennsylvania), Le Boef and Presque Isle were overcome by subterfuge. In most of the situations the surrendering soldiers were tortured and killed. Like Fort Detroit, Fort Pitt held out.

The British retaliated by giving small pox infected blankets to counseling chiefs. Such an act did not seem to infect them. The disease was already spreading across Ohio Country. An attack on a relief column for Fort Pitt was repulsed at the Battle of Bushy Run and the siege was broken. On the other hand, near Fort Niagra, a supply train was attacked as well as the relief column. The battle was called the Devil's Hole Massacre.

(Side Bar) The American film industry cannot be depended on to portray history. For example. C.B. De Mille produced a 1947 epic *Unconquered*. Based on Neil H. Swanson's novel *The Judas Tree*, 1933. Pontiac's combined Indian tribes lay waste to the Ohio Country killing settlers and overcoming forts. The bad Indian chief Guyasuta (Kiyasuta), played by Boris Karloff, is fooled by

Gary Cooper (Cpt. Christopher Holden) rescuing Paulette Goddard (Abby), an indentured servant, from torture and death. The film is a poor representation of the novel. For example, the end overlooks the defining Battle of Bushy Run claimed as one of the great British victories assuaging Braddock's defeat. The siege of Fort Pitt is lifted by Holden, who was condemned to death for desertion, using dead British soldiers killed at the Battle of Bushy Run. There is no evidence that such a ruse ever happened or that Guyasuta was there. He has equal prominence with George Washington at Point State Park in Pittsburgh.

A gang of Pennsylvania colonists from the village of Paxton took out their frustrations on innocent, Christian Indians at Conestoga in December. These "Paxton Boys" then headed for Philadelphia but were stopped by a militia put together by Benjamin Franklin. Indian massacres of settlers occurred as far as Virginia. In Franklin County Pennsylvania, Indians invaded a school house and killed and scalped the teacher and students. Two children survived the Enoch Brown massacre. The county today is famous for the discovery of oil: Oil City.

By August 1764, the violence had burned itself out. The Indian agent made a partial peace at Fort Niagra. Then Colonel John Bradstreet was sent to subdue the remaining Indians. Instead he made unauthorized peace agreements.

The Ohio Country Indians agreed to return captives from this and the French and Indian War. Pontiac signed a peace of sorts at Fort Ontario in July 1766. He was killed by another Indian some years later. The British/Indian relations went back to the way they were. Some historians use the term ethnic cleansing to describe the actions of the colonists and the Indians. The colonists ignored the Indian Reserve boundary and the Indian resentment continued to fester into the Revolutionary War.

Lord Dunmore's War was a prelude to the Revolutionary War in the Indian territories. Shawnee and Mingo tribes, claiming the land south of the Ohio River, ran into white incursions. Daniel Boone and his family were one group of invaders ignoring the Treaty of Fort Stanwix. A white massacre of intoxicated Indians at Yellow Creek (Ohio) inflamed the situation.

Gary Nash tells a different story of Virginians massacring women and children in a canoe on the Ohio River. John Logan, a half-French, half-Mingo war-leader retaliated since these were his relatives. Settlers raced for shelter. The British royal governor of Virginia sent out the militia to put down the tribes.

Chiefs Cornstalk and Blue Jacket attacked a force at Point Pleasant (West Virginia) and, after, a day long battle (1774) retreated across the Ohio. The ensuing peace was brief before hostilities began again. Now Kentucky was wide open for speculation by Dunmore and the Virginia elite according to Nash.

The Ohio Indian Wars or the Northwest Indian War

Between the end of the Revolutionary War and the War of 1812, the Ohio Country hardly remained quiet. From April through December of 1790, settlers were attacked in several incidents.

Potawatomis, Miamis, Delawares, and Shawnees massacred settlers near Stackport in southern Ohio in 1791. The massacre is memorialized at the Big Bottom State Monument. In November of that year, the greatest defeat of the American Army by Indians occurred on the banks of the Wabash River. The well-planned attacks were led by Blue Jacket, a Shawnee Indian. This defeat led to American militia massacring unarmed Delawares at Schoenbrunn village near New Philadelphia, Ohio. A museum memorializes that site as well. At the site of the defeat on the Wabash River, Anthony Wayne built Fort Recovery and withstood two days of attack in 1794 to end the resistance.

These incursions led to the **Battle of Fallen Timbers**, August 20, 1794. This final battle of the Northwest Indian War, was fought 3/4 mile north of the banks of the Maumee River. The

Indians under the leadership of Blue Jacket, believing that the wind toppled trees would be protective, were overwhelmed by a much larger militia including calvary. They retreated to British held Fort Miami but the British did not want to start an incident that might lead to war and refused their protection. Today the battlefield and Fort Miami are just south of alternate U.S. 20. General Wayne signed the Treaty of Green Ville near present day Greenville, Ohio in 1795.

After this decisive victory for General Anthony Wayne, all of the greater Maumee River Valley area was ceded to the United States. Prior to the development of canals, portages between the rivers were important trade routes and were safeguarded by forts such as Fort Loramie, Forts Recovery and Defiance at the junction of Maumee with Auglaize and Tiffin Rivers. In honor of General Wayne's victory on the banks of the Maumee, the primary bridge crossing the river near downtown Toledo is the Anthony Wayne Suspension Bridge. The Maumee River runs from Fort Wayne to Toledo.

The area remained relatively calm until the prelude to the War of 1812 of which we will see more of in the next chapter.

Defining Ohio Country and the United States

"And no man now thought he could live except he had catle and a great deale of ground to keep them all, all striving to increase their stocks. By which means they were scattered all over the bay quickly and the towne in which they lived compactly till now was left very thinne." Governor

William Bradford about the Plymouth colony quoted in *Measuring America*, p 35.

Before the American Revolution, land ownership was defined by "metes and bounds" using the natural features as identifying markers. Unfortunately, there were no standard linear measures. Personal ownership of land was a new concept. The land was nominally owned by the king. For example, that land Bradford was writing about was owned by the British monarchy. In 1763, King George III could decree the boundary of settlement at the Appalachians and any settlement farther was prohibited. This did not prevent the race for land across those mountains.

Opening up of Ohio Country following the war challenged the Continental Congress to measure this government land before the expected influx of settlers and speculators. Thomas Jefferson, successful in defining the American dollar in decimals, wanted a metric system of weights and measures as was being established in France. He was supported by Washington, Madison, Monroe and Hamilton. But Congress dithered until finally it was forced to decide on the Gunter chain of 22 yards to measure the new land: 10 chains a furlong; 80 chains a mile; 480 chains one side of a township. Jefferson got his squares to define the remainder of America but they would be in yards not meters.

The survey of Ohio Country began on the Ohio River September 30, 1785. Indian raids until the Battle of Fallen Timbers would slow the speculators long enough for Congress to act. Nevertheless, this first survey ending in 1787, was sloppy at best made worst by the fact that some of the surveyors were employed by land speculators. One speculator, Reverend Manasseh Cutler bought land at 12 cents an acre for the Ohio Company. Most of the land would be bought with script used to pay the soldiers and the states for the war.

Fortunately, the 1787 ordinance passed by Congress defining the measurement of this Northwest Territory allowed one section in each township set aside for education.

Freedom of religion and prohibition of slavery were also established 80 years before the 13th Amendment and three years before the U.S. Constitution was adopted.

In 1788, The first permanent settlement was established at what is now Marietta, Ohio, in a county appropriately named Washington. The squares, in reality, were so far out of square so as to make a carpenter cry and resulted in much confusion about boundaries and ownership. If the squares of Ohio looked like a Dali landscape, the surveying of Indiana from Ohio's western boarder looked like a checkered table cloth with straight north-south meridians.

Geographer Hidegard B. Johnson wrote in 1976: "The magnitude of the greatest land-measurement project in history is mind-boggling." Considering the problems met by trying to chain straight lines through virgin forests and the hills and valleys sculpted by the glaciers with the tools of the time, it *is* mind-boggling.

Thus, America was expanded by speculators, many in high office, in some of the most spectacular land grabs in history. For example, Moses Cleaveland, surveyor and major stockholder in the Connecticut Land Company, acquired the 3.5-million-acre Western Reserve. Just when the expansion appeared over, Jefferson purchased the Louisiana Territory. The squaring of the United States would continue, as Jefferson dreamed, all the way to the Pacific Ocean.

I have relied on Andro Linklater's *Measuring America* for this story.

The Civil War

Although it is not on our route, the incursion of John Hunt Morgan and his horse soldiers during the Civil War is worth taking time to savor. Beginning July 2, 1863, Morgan led more than 2,000 troopers from Kentucky across the Ohio River into southern Indiana and Ohio destroying railroad transportation and burning and looting Indiana towns of Corydon, Salem, Vienna, Livington, Vernon, and Versailles. Crossing into Ohio at Harrison, he bamboozled the garrisons at Cincinnati and Hamilton to retain their troops. But the chase began. He was caught with his back against the Ohio River at Buffington Island. Only 330 men made it across the river. Morgan led the remainder out of the trap zigzagging toward Nelsonville, Ohio. He was captured near West Point, Ohio, and incarcerated in the Ohio State Penitentiary in Cincinnati. He escaped by digging his way out and made it south to fight again.

His exploits gave the Confederacy some joy after the losses at Gettysburg and Vicksburg and probably kept a sufficient number of Federal troops engaged to change the outcome of the Battle of Chickamauga. I include this vignette to remind us that there were incursions into the North other than Antietam and Gettysburg during the Civil War.

CHAPTER FIVE:
INDIANA

Statehood 1816

Concerning the lines separating Indians and settlers: "The Indians urge this; The Law requires it; and it ought to be done; but I believe scarcely anything short of a Chinese Wall, or a line of Troops will restrain Land Jobbers, and the Incroachment [sic] of Settlers, upon the Indian Territory." George Washington, 1796 quoted in *The Legacy of Conquest* p 192

The boundaries of Indiana territory were set by congress in 1809. It was settled first by Kentucks and Virginians rather than New Englanders. Virginian William Henry Harrison permitted slavery as governor. Nevertheless, after vigorous opposition, the state constitution prohibited slavery with the tacit assumption that Blacks were not expected in the state.

The first city of interest along highway 20 in Indiana is **Angola**, population 7,344 at the 2000 census. There are several sites on the National Historic Register including the Steuben County Courthouse (1850), The Free Church also known as the Powers Church (1825), and the CCC Shelter in Pokagon State Park. The traffic circle in the town's center hosts a memorial to Civil War soldiers. Angola is also home to Tri-State University.

Likewise, the LaGrange County Courthouse (1875) in **La Grange**, population 2,919, is on the National Register. The county is also Amish Country with several locations to shop for authentic goods particularly in Shipshewana. The traveler should be aware that much of the goods sold at the commercial establishments are not authentically Amish.

After La Grange, 20 skirts south of South Bend and continues on state road 2 and U.S. 20 to Rolling Prairie, Springeville, and Michigan City.

It is worth a side trip into **South Bend** if for no other reason than to visit the University of Notre Dame. The city contains many sites on the National Register including the university. If the traveler leaves the four-lane-like 20 and takes business 20, it goes into **Elkhart**. The town's downtown is a historic district as well as are several private homes. Then continue to South Bend and north on 393 to the University. The basilica and the grotto are worth visiting as well as experiencing the ambience of the buildings and lake.

(Side Bar) Downtown South Bend is also the site of the Studebaker National Museum. The brother's blacksmith shop opened in 1852 and became the Studebaker Manufacturing Company in 1868 making wagons. The company introduced an electric car in 1902 followed by a gasoline-powered one in 1904. The first cars of the Studebaker Corporation were made in Detroit. In 1920, production was moved to South Bend. During the Second World War the company had several military contracts including the B-17 Flying Fortress engines. Apparently the company was too forward looking to compete with the Detroit companies. The present museum is located on the corner of Thomas and Chapen Streets. There is an admission.

After leaving South Bend the traveler enters the Chicago metropolitan area. **Michigan City,** population 32,900, in La Porte County is noted for both its proximity to the Indiana Dunes National Lakeshore and for its bordering Lake Michigan. Because of this, Michigan City receives a fair amount of tourism during the summer months, especially by residents of Chicago and parts of Indiana. The Muskegon Shipwreck Site and the Lighthouse (built in 1858) in Washington Park are on the National Register. The dunes are on U.S. 12. If you go northeast away from the dunes, the traveler can visit Long Beach and contrast the elegant homes along the beach with the natural beauty of the dunes preserved for the enjoyment of all.

To avoid the congestion around **Chicago**, this section of travel stops at the dunes.

The War of 1812 in the northwest territories really began with the battle at Tippecanoe. Governor of Indiana Territory since 1801, William Henry Harrison entered disputed Indian lands in late 1811 and established Fort Harrison at present day Terre Haute. At camp on the Vermillion River, Tecumseh's band under the direction of his brother, The Prophet, attacked before dawn and was repulsed due to some bravery by Harrison. Prophetstown was abandoned and ransacked by the Americans. The result was the banishment of The Prophet by Tecumseh and his "eternal hatred of the whites." The Tippecanoe Battlefield is right off I-65 north of Lafayett, Indiana.

Due to incompetent leadership by Governor of Michigan Territory, William Hull, Tecumseh's forays led to the surrender of Detroit in the summer of 1812, then Fort Dearborn followed by the massacre of the inhabitants. Harrison was directed by

President Madison to retake Detroit and most of the next two years was spent on that attempt.

But first, Tecumseh led the attack and massacre at Pigeons Roost, Indiana. He then attacked Fort Harrison which was under the command of Captain Zachary Taylor. The blockhouse was burned, but Taylor rallied the troops and held off the Indian attacks until a relief column arrived 13 days later. Tecumseh then attacked Fort Wayne which was relieved by Harrison. In retribution for Tecumseh's attacks, Indian towns were ransacked on the Auglaize River, at Elkhart and on the Wabash River. The Auglaize River is a tributary of the Maumee River, approximately 100 miles long, in northwestern Ohio

Winter campaigning 1812-1813 led to one disaster after another from the area around Detroit to Niagra Falls. Supply difficulties kept the soldiers in dire straits and typhus spread in the miserable mobs.

It was a war of rivers and lakes. Militia would not cross into Canada to fight the British and Indians. Winfield Scott lost an attack across the Niagra River with his artillery because militia would not come to his aid and the British maneuvered better. Sloppy leadership of General James Winchester led to the massacre on the River Raisin, Frenchtown, Michigan. This seemed to end military engagements until Perry's victory on lake Erie.

Both adversaries had to build their own fleets of warships on the Great Lakes and supply them with guns. Oliver H. Perry got lucky dragging his ships over a sandbar into Lake Erie under the eye of the enemy. Once there he bravely met the enemy and finally captured him losing his flagship in the battle. With American control of the lake, the British forts could not be supplied so they withdrew from Amherstburg, on the Detroit River in Ontario.

In April 1813, the British force from Detroit laid siege to Fort Meigs, located across the Maumee River from the site of the Battle of Fallen Timbers. The British and Tecumsah's Indians inflicted heavy losses on the ill-trained Americans. Nevertheless, the fort held out and the failure of the siege prevented British further incursion into the Ohio valley. The reconstructed fort and museum are located near Perrysburg, Ohio, off of highway 20 on state route 65.

The abandonment of the British forts along Lake Erie allowed Harrison to invade Canada. Outside of Detroit, The Battle of the Thames was won with a charge by Kentucky calvary. Tecumseh was killed.

On the Niagara River, Winfield Scott redeemed his honor at the Battle of Chippewa, July 5, 1814 and the Battle of Niagara Falls, July 25. The war sputtered to a close like two worn-out boxers in a perpetual clinch. Peace talks had been going on for over a year. Briton had to remain focused on France. So both agreed to the Treaty of Ghent where each did not get the concessions that they had fought over. Then another future president smashed the British Redcoats at New Orleans.

George Rogers Clark in the Revolution

The British lieutenant governor Henry Hamilton, at Fort Detroit, encouraged the Indians to raid settlements in Kentucky. George Rogers Clark reasoned that the best way to end these incursions was to destroy the British forts in the Ohio Valley. The Kentucky governor, Patrick Henry, sent him to do the job.

In July 1778, Clark's small band of 175 men took control of Kankaskia on the shore of the Mississippi River in southern Illinois. He then captured Vincennes. The towns were formerly French controlled and not inclined to serve the British. Several other Indian villages were also taken. Vincennes is located on the Illinois River on the Indiana side. It was briefly the capital of Indiana Territory as Kankaskia was of Illinois Territory.

When Hamilton reocupied Vincennes, Clark returned in February 1779, to retake the town and capture Hamilton. He convinced the fort to surrender by executing five

Indians in front of the British. This was the highlight of Clark's fame. In August 1780, Clark won a victory near present day Spring Field. Then he tried to capture Detroit but didn't succeed.

In 1782, he was not present at the Battle of Blue Licks which destroyed about 100 Kentucky militia and is considered the last battle of the Revolution. Present were Daniel Boone and one of his sons who was killed. The battle field state park lies south east of Cincinnati.

Clark retaliated destroying several Indian villages along the Great Miami River. A young Black Hawk (see the Black Hawk War, 1832, in the next volume) watched this and recalled that it was that moment when he developed his hatred for the Americans.

CHAPTER SIX:

ILLINOIS

Statehood 1818

"Fires took a dozen lives a day. In describing the fire dead, the term the newspapers most liked to use was "roasted." There was diphtheria, typhus, cholera, influenza. And there was murder. In the time of the fair the rate at which men and women killed one another rose sharply throughout the nation but especially in Chicago, where police found them selves without the manpower or expertise to manage the volume. In the first six months of 1892 the city experienced nearly eight hundred violent deaths. Four a day. Most were prosaic, arising from robbery, argument, or sexual jealousy. Men shot women, women shot men, and children shot one another by accident.' *The Devil in the White City* by Erik Larsson p 12

Since I spend a large chapter in the next volume on Illinois, I will be brief here reminding the reader of the early history of Chicago. As the Native Americans were pushed farther west, the Potawatomis replaced the Miami, Sauk and Fox. In 1770, a trading post was established on the Des Plaines River which empties into Lake Michigan. The army built Fort Dearborn there in 1803. During the War of 1812 the fort was abandoned upon agreement with the British. The escaping soldiers, women and children were killed or captured by the Potawatomis. The British ransomed the captives and freed the survivors. After the war, a town quickly grew on the mud flats and was incorporated in 1837.

The state's name is a Frenchafied Indian word for "the men." At the same time Indiana was set as a territory, Illinois was designated as such. It was also populated by southern emigrants. In 1823, a near civil war broke out over holding slaves. Slavery lost according to Walter McDougall because the majority of people did not want Blacks in the state.

In spite of the fact that I was born in Chicago, I want to hold true to my decision to bi-pass the major cities whenever possible. This toddlen' town of Carl Sandberg, Upton Sinclair, Al Capone, and Frank Sinatra kept me coming back after my parents escaped the violence before I had developed any lasting memories. My mother told me that she pushed me around what remained of the fair grounds. I have returned as a teen and again to present papers at scientific conventions.

Nevertheless, I must point out one of the major historical events in America of the 19th century occurred in the Windy City: The Chicago World's Fair and Columbian Exposition. It is, and was, an accomplishment of superlatives that almost never happened and was too soon forgotten history.

This town, built on the mud and sand many feet thick, grew bold in spite of a great fire in 1871, or maybe because of it. By 1890, it had decided to surpass the Paris exposition of 1889 and create a modern marvel of architectural and structural engineering. Called the White City, it succeeded in spite of overwhelming odds. Among many of the innovations it introduced was electric lighting and the first Ferris wheel which was to out Eiffel the Eiffel Tower. Many of the buildings burned to the ground soon after the closing.

As a side note, Buffalo Bill's Wild West show, although not part of the exposition, drew huge crowds. At one point Bill Cody made a grand gesture to Susan B. Anthony whom he invited to his show. The horse race from Chadron, Wyoming (see volume II) ended at the show. Later it was learned that the winner of the prize had put himself and his horse on a train and rode part of the way. I do recommend the Larsson book quoted above.

CHAPTER SEVEN:
LESSER KNOWN

Mary Dyer (1611-1660) was a strong advocate for women's rights and religious freedom. She arrived from England with her husband in the colony of Massachusetts in 1635. She soon became friends with Anne Hutchinson and was penalized for the association. They were banished in 1638 upon the discovery of the birth of a deformed fetus. It had been secretly buried because the Puritans would punish the parents for their sins. A deformed fetus was one sign of sinfullness. The family migrated to land occupied by Roger Williams and eventually began farming for the third time in New Port, Rhode Island.

The family traveled to England with Roger Williams in 1652. There she met Margaret Fell (another strong advocate of women's rights) and the founder of the Religious Society of Friends (Quakers). She became a Quaker minister and stayed away from her family five years. Quaker teaching resonated with what she had learned with Anne Hutchinson. Upon returning to Boston, she was confined without communication for two months not hearing that Quakers were banned from Boston. Her husband rescued her by agreeing that she would not return to Massachusetts.

She began forming Quaker meetings throughout New England holding some with slaves and Indians. Nevertheless, she visited Quakers imprisoned in Boston again. The Puritans ordered that Quakers returning to the city would be banished upon pain of death. She was imprisoned and taken to the Boston Common to be hung. The two men were hung. She was reprieved at the last moment. Upon a third visit, she was convicted and hung on the Common in 1660. Her death resulted in Charles II admonishing Governor John Endicott never to do it again and send Quakers back to England for any trials. The king eventually signed the Rhode Island Charter which contained a stipulation for freedom of religion (1663). That freedom would eventually appear in the first article of the Bill of Rights to the Constitution.

Robert Rogers (1727?-1795) Captain Robert Rogers from New Hampshire is responsible for the ranger concept that is still used for military small reconnaissance tactics. He held land in the disputed Hampshire Grants. When the French and Indian War started, he was recruited by the British for spying out the French forts. He formed a backwoods crew of fighters called Roger's Rangers that raided along the Hudson Valley and Lake Champlain using Indians and freed slaves in his band. Located at Fort William Henry he harassed French at Forts Ticonderoga and Crown Point. In Canada, he ranged from Montreal to Quebec with Wolfe's and Amherst's expeditions. He traveled through present day Cleveland meeting Pontiac before establishing British presence in Detroit.

Rogers was also sent to fight the Cherokees in South Carolina and was also at the Battle of Bloody Ridge (1763).

After the war, he was appointed to an area in upper Michigan but was accused of high treason in 1768 for mismanagement of funds and sent to England for a court-martial trial. In London, he was acquitted and then tried to get money and a knighthood for his accomplishments during the war.

At the beginning of the Revolution, he tried to get an appointment from Washington but was rejected for fear that he was a Tory spy. He then joined the British as an officer. Defeated at the Mameronee, New York (1776), he headed back to England. [Most of this biography comes from a history published in 1885 in Boston.]

Benjamin Edes 1732-1803 was as responsible as some of the better-known Patriots for planting the seeds of the rebellion. With the vindication of John Peter Zinger for seditious libel for printing what someone else wrote in 1735, newspapers became the internet blogs of the time. Edes, as publisher of the Boston *Gazette*, published tracts from Samuel Adams, James Otis and Joseph Warren. Raul Revere engraved the *Gazette* masthead. As the British rule became more oppressive, the attacks in print became more outrageous, some of it true. John Adams convinced Edes to change the masthead to "A free press maintains the majesty of the people."

The liberty pot bubbled over in 1770 when Samuel Adams and Paul Revere "turned the shooting of five rioting civilians into the 'Boston Massacre.'" [from *Back Issues* "the day the newspaper died," *The New Yorker*, January 26, 2009 page 71] Edes was one of many on the British list to be killed when war came. It was at the Edes home that the men collected, drank punch, dressed as Indians, and headed to the Boston Tea Party according to Edes's son Peter who was among 2000 observers to the tea dump.

When Lexington and Concord occurred, Edes packed up his press and carried it across the Charles River to Watertown where he continued to print the *Gazatte*. The British took Edes's son prisoner when they couldn't find the father. After the war, Edes was a Whig in a Federalist stronghold and fought with his former friend John Adams. In reply to the attacks on Adams as president including those by Thomas Jefferson, Adams had the Sedition Act passed in Congress silencing his detractors. Edes went out of business and died destitute three years after Jefferson's Inauguration.

Native American **Joseph Brant** is one important figure before, during, and after the Revolutionary War that few have heard of. He and his sister, Molly, could be considered wards of Sir William Johnson, Royal Superintendent of Indian Affairs for the region that is now New York. He was educated to be a missionary but returned to his people to be treated as a chief due to his negotiating skills. He became a prosperous farmer before the Revolution. When General Gage withdrew the British troops to Boston, the frontier exploded. Brant trusted the British to protect Iroquois lands from Patriot incursion.

When Benedict Arnold and Ethan Allen began an unauthorized campaign and captured Fort Ticonderoga and Crown Point, Brant felt his relatives in the Mohawk Valley were in danger and headed for Canada. His wife and child were kept as prisoners.

A visit to England, to protest the colonists' treatment of the Mohawks, where he was treated as a celebrity, he returned to find the Revolution had begun. He convinced several tribes in Oswego, in 1777, including the Seneca to join the British. He led several attacks on settlements and joined the attack on Fort Stanwix and the Battle of Oriskany.

Brant was joined by John Butler, a Loyalist, and more than 500 immigrants from the New York area. Later this mixed group of Indians from several tribes along with Loyalists out maneuvered the defenders of Forty Fort in the Wyoming Valley. The ensuing massacre became a cause celebre for the patriots.

The patriots burned several villages including Brant's. In retaliation Brant and Butler attacked villages in Cherry Valley (1778). Then Washington sent the Sullivan expedition to wipe out the Indians in New York. This back and forth retribution continued until there was nothing left to destroy. An angry Brant walked out of the Fort Stanwix treaty of 1784. The fate of the tribes east of the Mississippi was obvious. Hatred of Indians would push the American states across the Mississippi into the Louisiana Purchase.

Brant established a colony and Brants Town on the Grand River in Canada but ran up against British authority attempting to control him. He moved back and forth across the boundary attempting to preserve Indian lands from encroachment. He visited

President Washington as well as returning to London to plead his case without apparent success. Speaking of a New York commissioner appointed to deal with Brant, Brant observed the he "would skin a flint if it was possible, should it belong to the Indians." Brant died at age 63 in 1807.

Nathaniel Greene (1742-1785) "We are soldiers who devote ourselves to arms not for the invasion of other countries, but for the defense of our own, not for the gratification of our private interests but for public security"

A fascinating, little-known hero of the Revolution, Greene was raised by Quaker parents in Rhode Island where he was treated as a celebrity, and was a blacksmith before the war. He was an avid Whig (Patriot) supporting the Declaration of Independence and organizing a militia. He was expelled from his Quaker Meeting for marrying a non-Quaker. Of course his military bent could have also contributed. He studied books on military science and tactics and jumped from private to brigadier general on Washington's staff. He designed the defenses of Long Island and took part in the battles of Trenton, Brandywine, Germantown. He served as the quartermaster general resigning that position in a fuss with the Continental Congress. A Freemason and Lafayette's friend, he was also at the battles of Monmoth (1718) and Springfield (1780) then presiding over the trial and sentencing of Major John André before becoming commander of West Point.

After several American generals had suffered losses in the South, he took command. Planning a strategic retreat, he enticed Cornwallis to a resounding defeat at Cowpens, North Carolina. By retreating farther across the Dan River he escaped the superior force. Finally, Cornwallis, in defeating Greene at Gulford Court House, lost so many men he was forced to retreat. The British were finally penned to the coast in North and South Carolina and Virginia.

He died in 1786 of heat stroke on his land near Savannah, Georgia. Sixteen states have Greene Counties and 15 cities are named for him, two in North Carolina.

Ethan Allen (1738-1789 A rebel before the American Revolution, Allen and his brothers were responsible for forming the state of Vermont. How his name became associated with high-end furniture is a mystery. His name did become a symbol for strength and daring.

It all began (1749) when the governor of New Hampshire made some grants of land from the Connecticut River across the Green Mountains approaching the Hudson River which the state of New York could have disputed at the time but didn't. When the land speculation was discovered, New York got King George III to grant the land to New York speculators. By 1770, the disputed land was in legal and mob turmoil. The brothers Allen had a financial stake in the speculation. Ethan Allen was the center of legal maneuvering and mob government called the Green Mountain Boys.

Farmers were working the Hampshire Grant land and any attempt for the "Yorkers" to remove them brought out the Green Mountain Boys. New York put a price on Allen's head. Then potential confrontation with the British brought the Green Mountain Boys and some militia to head toward Fort Ticonderoga before the Yorkers could. Benedict Arnold, with a commission from the Massachusetts Committee of Safety, also headed for the fort. In his splendid uniform, diminutive Arnold did not go over well with Allen and the boys. He was allowed to go along when they took the fort with one shot in May 1775. The British guns were collected by Arnold and held at Lake George until sent to Boston.

Allen headed to Montreal to capture the city but supporting troops failed him and he was captured. He endured three years of bad and worse treatment by the British, who sent him to England, and then to the Tories in this country. Meanwhile, the Allen brothers minus Ethan were building the state of Vermont. Ticonderoga had fallen allowing Burgoyne to head for Albany. Part of his army was defeated at the Battle of Bennington with the Green Mountain Militia in the middle of it.

During the rest of the Revolution, the area which was to become Vermont (French for Green Mountain) was in a civil war sometimes between the residents east and west of the Green Mountains and sometimes with Yorkers. At one time, the Allen brothers were in conversations with the British to rejoin the empire playing off the Continental Congress against the British. Congress would not recognize Vermont as a state.

After the war, Allen became heavily involved in land speculation. In spite of a minimal education, Ethan Allen was a well-spoken author of books, legal papers and documents and could rouse a gathering to action. He died of a cerebral hemorrhage in 1789 and did not live to see Vermont become a state in 1791.

Joseph Warren (1741-1775) Graduate of Harvard, Warren studied and practiced medicine, was Grand Master of the Freemasons of Boston and member of the Sons of Liberty with Sam Adams and John Hancock. He preformed the autopsy on a young rabble rouser killed by a customs service employee defending his home. The boy's death brought on the Boston Massacre 11 days later.

Outspoken and well-written about the British oppression, he was president of the Massachusetts Provincial Congress. He sent William Daws and Paul Revere on their Midnight Ride and took part in chasing the British back from Lexington and Concord and in the Siege of Boston. He was killed by a British office with a shot to the back of his head during the last British charge at Bunker Hill. His brother went on to act a surgeon to the army during the war and took part in establishing the Harvard Medical School.

Anthony Wayne (1745-1796) A Pennsylvania surveyor for himself and others including Benjamin Franklin, he was appointed a Colonel in the 4th Pennsylvania Regiment which took part in the disastrous invasion of Canada during the Revolution. He commanded forces at Fort Ticonderoga before it was retaken by the British. He then fought at the battles at Brandywine, Paoli, Germantown and Monmouth. He then led a nighttime bayonet attack taking Stony Point on the Hudson River. The victory gave the Patriots some hope after the series of losses. On the way to West Point, he punished a recalcitrant soldier with lashes. The man shouted "Mad Anthony Wayne" and the label stuck.

Victorious at West Point and Green Spring Virginia, he negotiated peace with the Creek and Cherokee Indians in Georgia. For this he was given land in Georgia where he lived until called back into service by Washington to put down the Indian uprisings in Ohio Country. He assaulted the Indian Confederacy at the Battle of Fallen Timbers with the professionally trained soldiers under his command which was called The Legion of the United States.

He died of gout and was buried first at Fort Presque Isle (Erie). His body was disinterred and his boiled bones placed in a saddle bag to the journey to Radnor, Pennsylvania taking the present U.S. 322. According to one story, some of the bones were lost along the way and his ghost searches for them on his birthday. There are 13 counties and at least 15 cities or towns named for him. Actor Marion Morrison was given the name John Wayne instead of Anthony Wayne.

Winfield Scott (1786-1866) His military service spanned the history of the United States from the War of 1812, as we have seen, to the Civil War. And yet, he is hardly mentioned today unless it is his Anaconda Plan to choke the Confederacy. He was too late to influence the Black Hawk war as will be seen in the next Book. He was used to put pressure on South Carolina to end its attempt to "nullify" a tariff putting hardship on southern planters. He was involved in the longest war between the Revolution and the Vietnam War: The Second Seminol War, 1835-42. During that period he was sent by President Andrew Jackson to Georgia to control the Cherokee Nation and eventually send them on the "Trail of Tears." The U.S. involvement in Spanish Florida and the suppression of the Seminoles, some of whom were black, is another shameful piece of American history. His slow invasion of Mexico (1847-48) ended at Chapultepec. He ran for president in 1852, but was defeated by Franklin Pierce. He defused the confrontation with the British over San Juan Island known as the "Pig War" (see Oregon in second volumn) in 1859. Robert E. Lee was under his command in Mexico. Both Virginians, he remained with the Union while Lee reluctantly went with Virginia. Too fat and feeble, for active service he resigned as general-in-chief in late 1861, but did live to see the end of the rebellion.

George Rogers Clark (1752-1818) Clark was from a large family raised on a large Virginia plantation. Like George Washington, he became a surveyor entering Kentucky on the Ohio River. He was a captain of Virginia militia during Lord Dunmore's War. During the Revolution, he convinced Governor Patrick Henry to extend Virginia by creating Kentucky County across the Appalachians.

Kentucky became a bloody battle ground with Native American raids. The Indians were supplied by the British lieutenant governor Henry Hamilton. Patrick Henry sent Clark to destroy the British forts in Illinois Country. Clark's exploits encouraged Washington and led Virginia to extend its boundaries to Illinois County giving claim to extending the 13 colonies into Ohio Country. (Virginia claimed all the land into Illinois based on the ambiguity of the original Royal Charter.)

Clark's life was at his zenith then and deteriorated due to later losses, such as Blue Licks, where he was commander but not present. During the Northwest Indian War, he presented a confusing record and was accused of being drunk on duty. He retired to land in present day Indiana that the government gave to him for his services.

A French plan to open up the Mississippi Valley by defeating the Spanish with Clark at the lead was stopped by President Washington. He lost most of his land to claims of lenders. He was part of a company, along with Arron Burr, planning to build a canal around the Falls of the Ohio near Louisville. The plan fell through when vice president Burr was arrested for treason for attempting to carry out the same plan to open up the Mississippi.

Clark's health deteriorated from drink, strokes and a leg amputation. He was cared for by his brother-in-law and his younger brother William Clark upon his return from his expedition with Meriwether Lewis. After Clark's death, his hero status was promoted.

Dwitt Clinton (1769-1828) After education at what is now Columbia University, Clinton served in various political capacities including the U.S. Senate from New York, then mayor of New York City. In 1812, he ran against James Madison for president. He won a special election for governor of New York and continued that position, with a short hiatus, until his death in office.

He was a member of the Erie Canal Commission from 1810 to 1824 and, as governor, was largely responsible for its construction. When it was finished, he opened it by sailing to Buffalo then back to New York City where he empted two casks containing Lake Erie water. Nine towns and five Counties are named for him.

Tecumseh (1768-1813) was a highly regarded Shawnee war chief whose wide travels over the country east of the Mississippi were an attempt to coalesce Native American opposition to western expansion. His father was killed during Lord Dunmore's War. When William Henry Harrison bamboozled some Indians to sell Ohio land that they didn't live on, Tecumseh protested and, with his brother, organized a resistance. He told Harrison, "No tribe has the right to sell, even to each other, much less to strangers.... Sell a country! Why not sell the air, the great sea, as well as the earth? Didn't the Great Spirit make them all for the use of his children?" And, "....the only way to stop this evil is for the red man to unite in claiming a common and equal right in the land, as it was first, and should be now, for it was never divided." While Tecumseh was away attempting to form confederations, his brother, The Profit, attacked Harrison at Tippicanoe and retreated after the loss.

During the War of 1812, Tecumseh assisted the British in the attack and surrender of Detroit. When Perry's victory made Detroit untenable, he protected the British retreat to the Thames Valley in Canada. He was killed there during the Battle of the Thames by Richard Mentor Johnson who was later elected vice president serving with Martin Van Buren. While Johnson is forgotten, Tecumseh is considered an American and Canadian hero with many ship and place names and the middle name of a Civil War General.

First Picture Panel

Hancock Shaker Village

Women's Rights Museum statues with traveling partner Judith Greenberg

Perry Monument, Presque Isle

Michigan City

EPILOGUE

"The antiquarian strives to bring back the past for the sake of the past; the historian strives to show the present to itself by revealing its origin from the past. The goal of the antiquarian is the dead past; the goal of the historian is the living present." Frederick Jackson Turner, 1891 The Significance of History in *The Early Writings of FJT*

America was built on the hope for a better life, a "pursuit of happiness," and a drive to attain that happiness by any means possible. Speculation from the beginning of the royal land grants to the invasion of Ohio Country, from the encroachment of Native American lands across the Alleghenies to the Louisiana Purchase, from the war with Mexico to the war with Spain drove the "manifest destiny" of the nation. Money was to be made. It was a transshipped model of English imperialism.

Walter A. McDougall opines in *Freedom Just Around the Corner* that "creative corruption" drove the rapid growth of the United States. We can thank the rise of capitalism, the enclosure of English public land (which continues today in the western states), and the rule of Elizabeth I for the eventual beachheads of entrepreneurship in Virginia, Maryland, New York, Massachusetts and Delaware (where Finish colonists taught the English how to build log cabins).

With this separation from the mother-country came a new independence. The colonists as early as the mid 17th century refused to follow laws passed by the English Parliament. The English Civil War separated the colonists further. The several French and Indian wars as part of the European Wars created more dissent.

There was also population pressure to expand westward. Commenting on the Massachusetts experience, David Hacket Fischer writes in *Albion's Seed: Four British Folkways in America,* p 17, "They multiplied at a rapid rate, doubling every generation for two centuries. Their numbers increased to 100,000 by 1700, to at least one million by 1800 . . . — all descended from 21,000 English emigrants who came to Massachusetts in the period from 1629 to 1640." I am the direct descendent of second generation, immigrant Patton brothers who each had eight and nine progeny during the 18th and 19th century after serving in the Revolution. While the conquest of the continent was touted as ordained by the Creator it was really conquered by procreation.

Of course, on this continent, the wars were a French-British struggle for land: The French for trade with the Native Americans, the British for speculation. A subplot involved a religious war between Catholics and Protestants. After Bloody Mary and James II, the English were rightfully wary of Catholic French intentions.

As we traveled through the more northern parts of the greatest change the world had seen to that time, we saw the remnants of this revolution. For the wars that preceded the American Revolution were just a prelude to the creation of a new democracy, not perfect but renewable. It gave hope to the "huddled masses yearning to be free." It overcame the pernicious aristocracy, the swindlers, the gentry, the wealthy many of whom resisted a split from the mother country. It proclaimed that all men are equal, only to amended that to equality of all religions (or none), all races, all women . . . ALL. It was a rebellion of the mob against the landed establishment only modified by a few reasonable patriots. Moreover it was a civil war fracturing every section of society, the poor, the wealthy, the slave and freed man and the Native Americans. Only in the next Civil War would the country be so divided.

While it may have been the Boston Tea Party that triggered the train of events leading to rebellion, there had been a similar seizure of a ship in Philadelphia in 1724. Rebellion forced the separate colonies to attempt some kind of confederation or they would "hang separately." Benjamin Franklin actually had proposed such a plan in response to the French and Indian war in 1754 at the Albany Conference. While the plan never got the attention it deserved, the land speculators jockeyed for advantage in acquiring Native American lands during the conference.

The final split with Britain was over "self-government," religious freedom, economic opportunity, and territorial growth according to McDougall. Reasons enough for wealthy merchants and land owners to put their wealth and their lives on the line. The rebellion became a "holy war" against a perceived corrupt Britain.

The rapid turnabout by France from an enemy to a strong supporter also changed opinions about Catholics particularly those in Maryland. Similarly, Thomas Paine's *Common Sense* gave the colonists a sense of "WE" for the first time. This sense of unity would eventually appear in the preamble to the Constitution: "We the People of the United States, in Order to form a more perfect Union, . . . "

The war fractured Pennsylvania into rebels and Quakers. And yet, former Quaker General Nathaniel Greene won the war for the rebels with his southern strategy after stalemate. He died of heatstroke a few years later.

After the war, as we have seen, the frontier moved west amoeba-like, confronting the British, the Native Americans, the Mexicans, and the Spanish. Efforts to protect the pioneers and expand the territory were fragmented. Without Continental Congress approval, speculators and state militias worked separately to promote expansion of the states. The 13 colonies began flying apart. Then came Shay's Rebellion waking up Washington and the Federalists into action. The approval of the new Constitution was a real cliff-hanger. With Virginia's ratification June 25, 1788, the document took effect. New York followed.

It would take another war to establish the United States as a respectable nation. Victories on Lakes Erie and Champlain ended the British threat from the north and the strength shown at New Orleans, even after the peace treaty had been signed, gave the nation some respect. Thus, ended nearly 150 years of intermittent war similar to the European experience. Such history must have flavored the aggressive psyche of the American soul as it pushed west. There was fertile land to be plowed by the farmer and by the evangelists of many brands. The itinerant preacher could plant the seeds among the pioneers to ripen into Baptists, Methodists as well as Scottish Presbyterians. My great, great-grandfather was one of those Presbyterian circuit riders carrying a double-barreled shotgun through Illinois and Missouri Territory in the 1840s. This New Yorker established a home near Albany, Missouri, in the northwestern corner. Such was the way west. And such is the imperialist history of the United States. [1]

WINNERS AND LOSERS

Unfortunately, the propositions that all men are "created equal" and had such rights as "life liberty and the pursuit of happiness" were not universal. To get the Constitution ratified compromises were imbedded in the document that left out the largest segment of the American population. There were still limits as to which white males could vote.

---

1 For full disclosure, I have relied heavily on *Freedom Just Around the Corner*, by Walter A. McDougall, and *The Unknown American Revolution* by Gary B. Nash for the editorial comments in the epilogue.

Although Abigail Adams admonished her husband more than once to "remember the ladies," the American men forgot them until 1920. It was hard for the African-Americans, slave and free, who heard the words of equality but did not experience it. As far as the Indians were concerned, Jefferson actually disparaged the Native Americans in the Declaration of Independence.

There was a constant and rightful fear that the slaves would revolt. There had been a few such incidents before the rebellion. During the Seven Years War slaves had escaped to the French. As early as 1737 Quaker Benjamin Lay brought his concerns over slavery before Philadelphia Quakers (The Religious Society of Friends). He was followed by John Woolman and Anthony Benezat. In 1774, the slave trade was formally ended in part because there were too many. Otherwise slavery became an embarrassment to whites who were demanding freedom themselves.

In Virginia at the cuff of the war, Lord Dunmore offered any slave reaching Williamsburg freedom for serving with the British. The result was what Nash calls "The Greatest Slave Revolt in History." The clash at Concord triggered the fear that a slave revolt would occur. That fear brought South Carolina into the revolution.

There were African-American heroes both slave and free. More is heard of the black soldiers who fought with Washington although he did not formally recognize their recruitment. Former Quaker Colonel Christopher Greene from Warwick, Road Island, led a "Black Regiment" through several battles. After five years of fighting only one-third of the former slaves were alive to taste their freedom.

Less is written about those who stayed with the British and had to flee to Florida or Canada following the peace. A black Colonel Tye led a gorilla band mixed with white Loyalists in New Jersey terrorizing the patriots. In the end, many slaves who had not died of disease in the crowded refugee camps went back to their patriot owners. Tory owners took theirs away on ships. Even freed slaves as well as freemen were captured in the north and sent back south.

Women found their voices during the Great Awakening speaking up for their spiritual rights, then for their own rights. This influenced the most famous African-American poet of the 18th century, Phillis Wheatley, praised in London more than in Boston. The women, the backbone of the resistance to the taxes before the revolution and the sustaining force during it, were also ignored. It was women who made the nonimportation movement work. They relearned how to do homespun cloth. When merchants raised their prices for greater profit, the women revolted in Boston and Philadelphia.

Finally, as we have seen in previous sections, the situation of the Native Americans only became worse.

Writing *The Wealth of Nations* at the same time the Declaration of Independence was published, Adam Smith wrote " . . . civil authority, so far as it is instituted for the security of property, is in reality instituted for the defense of the rich against the poor, or of those who have some property against those who have none at all." Today there remains the same tension between those who have made gain from the sweat-labors of others and those others who see that wealth and the attendant power as ill-gotten gains. Equality remains the American Dream.

changes in county population in 10 years

African-Americans

County	squ mi	/squ mi	%Whites	%	Major City On 20	% change**
Suffolk, MA	120	11,692	58	22	Boston	3.4
Middlesex	848	1780	86	3	Marlborough	0.5
Worcester	1579	496	90	3	Sturbridge	4.2
Hampden	634	738	78	*	Springfield	0.4

County	squ mi	/squ mi	%Whites	%	Major City On 20	% change**
Berkshire	936	145	95	2	Pittsfield	-3.8
Columbia, NY	848	98	93	4	New Lebanon	-1.2
Albany	533	562	83	11	Albany	1.6
Schenectady	210	712	88	7	Duanesburg	2.9
Schoharie	626	52	97	1	Carlisle	1.5
Otsego	1003	62	96	2	East Springfield	1.2
Madison	662	44	96	1	Cezenova	0.6
Onondaga	806	588	85	9	Cardiff	-0.9
Cayuga	864	118	93	4	Auburn	-2.3
Seneca	325	103	95	2	Seneca Falls	2.7
Ontario	662	155	95	2	Geneva	3.7
Wyoming	595	73	92	5	Warsaw	-3.4
Erie	1227	909	82	13	Orchard Park	-3.9
Chautauqua	1500	65	94	2	Fredonia	-4.2
Erie, PA	1558	350	91	6	Erie	-0.6
Ashtabula, OH	1368	145	94	3	Ashtabula	-1.5
Lake	979	997	95	2	Mentor	2.6
Cuyahoga	1246	3040	67	27	Cleveland	-7.0

County	squ mi	/squ mi	%Whites	%	Major City On 20	% change**
Lorain	923	578	85	16	Oberlin	6.2
Huron	495	121	96	1	Norwalk	0.5
Sandusky	418	151	92	3	Bellview	-1.3
Wood	621	196	95	1	Perrysburg	3.6
Lucas	596	1337	77	17	Toledo	-2.9
Fulton (Alt 20)	407	104	96	*	Burlington	1.1
Williams	423	93	96	*	West Unity	-2.1
Steuben, IN	322	108	97	*	Angola	0.7
LaGrange	387	34	97	*	LaGrange	6.1
Elkhart	468	394	86	5	Elkhart	8.3
St Joseph	461	580	82	11	South Bend	0.2
LaPorte	613	184	86	10	Michigan City	-0.3
Porter	522	384	95	1	Portage	9.4
Lake	626	990	67	25	Gary	1.6

* Less than 1 percent ** from 2000 to 2007 from seattlepi.com

Sources

The War of 1812, John K. Mahon, 1972

After Tippecanoe: Some Aspects of the War of 1812, Philip P. Mason, 1963

Revoluntionary New England, James Truslow Adams,

Mary Dyer, Biography of a Rebel Quaker, Ruth Plimpton, 1995

The Cousin's Wars Religion, Politics , and the Triumph of Anglo-America, Keven Philips, 1999

Turncoats, Traitors, and Heroes, John Bakeless, 1959

Empires at War, William M. Fowler Jr.,

Those damn Horse Soldiers, George Walsh, 2006

Beyond Conquest Native Peoples and the Struggle for History in New England, Amy E. Ouden, 2005

Reinterpreting New England Indians and the Colonial Experience, Colen G. Calloway & Neal Salisbury, eds. 2003

Mayflower, Nathaniel Philbrick, 2006

The Invasion of America, Indians, Colonialism, and the Cant of Conquest, Francis Jennings, 1975

The Legacy of Conquest, Patricia N. Limerick, 1987

Indian War Sites: A Guide Book to Battlefields, Monuments, and Memorials, State by State with Canada and Mexico, Steve Rajtar,

Roadside Geology of New York, Bradford B.Van Diver, 1985

Roadside Geology of Massachusetts, James W. Skehan, 2001, unfortunately the author follows I-90

Roadside Geology of Pennsylvania, Bradford B. Van Diver, 1990, unfortunately the author follows I-90

Roadside Geology of Ohio, Mark J. Camp, 2006

Measuring America, Andro Linklater, 2002

Freedom Just Around the Corner, Walter A. McDougall, 2004

Bound for Canaan, Fergus M. Bordewich, 2005

The Unknown American Revolution, GarY B.Nash, 2005

River-Horse, William Least Heat-Moon, 1999

America's Hidden History, Kenneth C. Davis, 2008

Seizing Destiny, Richard Kluger, 2007

www.nationalregisterofhistoric places.com

The Damndest Yankees Ethan Allen and Hi Clan, Edwin P. Hoyt, 1976

The Divided Ground, Alan Taylor, 2006

VOLUME II

ROCKFORD, ILLINOIS, to NEWPORT, OREGON

ON U.S. 20

Mountain men, explorers, cowmen, troopers, emigrants, Indians, farmers and the topography of their lives

CONTENTS

VOLUME II ROCKFORD, ILLINOIS, to NEWPORT, OREGON	**97**
INTRODUCTION	**101**
CHAPTER ONE: ILLINOIS (1818)*	**107**
CHAPTER TWO: IOWA (1846)	**124**
CHAPTER THREE: NEBRASKA (1876)	**133**
CHAPTER FOUR: WYOMING (1890)	**153**
CHAPTER FIVE: IDAHO (1890)	**169**
CHAPTER SIX: OREGON (1859)	**183**
CHAPTER SEVEN: CROSSING THE EXPLORERS' TRAILS	**191**
EPILOGUE	**211**
SOURCES	**223**

INTRODUCTION

"... land was marginal, the climate inhospitable, the cultural amenities scarce, and the population insufficient to attract the infrastructure necessary to sustain or jump-start the cycle of regional growth." Promised Land, David M. Wrobel, 2002, p73

The route of U.S. highway 20 from Rockford, Illinois, to the Pacific exposes a record of westward migration little recognized by contemporary narratives. Railroads were much more prominent than wagon wheels traveling the Overland or Santa Fé routes. Emigrants were deposited at the end of the rails.

In preparation for this flood of pioneers, mapping expeditions were guided by former trappers. Forts were built for protection from Native Americans who were being pushed constantly farther west. Cattlemen sent their hoofed meat back east. "Manifest Destiny" was played out here as well as along the other routes to the West Coast.

Traveling this route is a modern "Voyage of Discovery" not quite as exciting as Lewis and Clark experienced but still full of surprises for the modern explorer who follows this trail of emigration. Volume one brought the traveler to the Chicago suburbs. This volume skips the Chicago web to find itself in Elmhurst and enters Rockford, Illinois, escaping from I-90 which will take a more northern route across the western half of the U.S. Highway 20 was commissioned in 1926 to go as far as Yellowstone National Park. In 1940, it continued to Albany, Oregon, and then finally to Newport, 3237 miles.

Along this line defined by U.S. 20, the westward migration of the pioneers was just as important as the more written-about trails and settlements. For example, the TIME-LIFE series *The Old West* ignores this corridor. "The Pioneers" volume emphasizes the Oregon Trail, the Mormon Trail and Kansas sod busters ignoring the northern portions of Illinois, Iowa and Nebraska. "The Cowboys" volume fails to mention the Sandhills and its own cattle-barons. I hope in some small way this volume fills in some of the missing history and creates an appreciation of this portion of the last "blue highway" crossing the continent.

This trek begins in land sculpted by a succeeding series of glaciers grinding rock, ripping up soil and depositing it in deep layers to be veined by rivers from the Great Lakes to the Rockies. Robert Douglas Mead, the author of *Heartland*, notes that the Midwest ". . . is, in fact, probably the most modified part of natural America. Of the 40 percent of Illinois that was once forest, only 12 percent remains wooded. Wetlands that once covered 30 percent of the state have now dwindled to only 3.5. Nearly 99 percent of the original prairie is gone."

As we approach the Rockies, the land becomes fractured by the up-thrusting of the earth's crust. Hot springs and foreboding volcanoes remind us of the fragility of the earth's surface. From the Rockies to the Pacific Ocean the land bares its naked geology in spectacular escarpments, jagged rock-castles and sleeping volcanoes.

The same types of players who populated the history of the better-known routes are seen along this corridor too. But, the topography along this highway made their experiences different. Here I have attempted to meld the topography with the history along U.S. 20.

The Illinois chapter begins outside of Chicago, the gateway to this westward expansion, at Rockford, Illinois. The completion of the Erie Canal, in 1825, allowed emigrants from New York to travel to Buffalo, then to Chicago, by ship. U.S. 20 heads nearly straight west making a slight detour to Yellowstone National Park. The route follows along the 42nd parallel from Rockford, Illinois, to Casper, Wyoming, before it loops up to Cody on the 44th, then down to Boise, Idaho, on the 43rd before ending at Newport on the 44th. Incidentally, U.S. 20 did acquire the name "the Yellowstone Highway." Wooden wheels and iron wheels cut this rout before the rubber hit the road.

In Illinois, the highway splits the scene of the tragic Black Hawk War where three future U.S. presidents chased the Indians. Native Americans first mined the lead near Galena, Illinois, before the white man came. But, nothing could stop the serge of settlers.

Crossing the Mississippi at Dubuque, Iowa, the land flattens out punctuated by silos, appearing like giant mushrooms, holding the grain for cattle more numerous than people. Just off the highway in Dyersville, rise the twin spires of one of the 32nd Basilica in the U.S. The Field of Dreams movie set is just a short trip through the town. Populated first by northern Europeans settling their family farms, this flatland is turning into corporate farms owned by nonresidents but still managed by farm families.

Further on, Fort Dodge preserves the military history of the relocation of the Native Americans. The culture of the horse is brought to life before the iron horse spread its contents even faster. The land becomes rolling as the highway approaches the Missouri River at Sioux City and the Lewis and Clark Integrative Center.

Nothing could stop the surge of settlers now as Nebraska opened up. The Ash Falls State Historical Park is a paleontologic dig exposing the bones of animals long gone from the state reminding us of the recent geologic history. Past the dig, real cowboy and Indian country unfolds. A museum of the fur trade presents a view of life and discovery before the press of civilization. A visit there prepares the reader for the travails of the mountain men and explorers as described in chapter seven.

Then the famous Sandhills surround the highway. Here the conflict between the cattlemen and the homesteaders became subject of Mari Sandoz stories and the source of many Hollywood films. Here also is another site of the subjugation and massacre of more Indians. Fort Robinson, on the highway, is a center for this history.

The culmination of this history so far is the Trails Museum in Casper, Wyoming. It depicts, in detail, the arduous journey that all the travelers took to explore and populate the West. After Casper the highway makes a loop to take in Yellowstone. This is wide-open country with as few as two people per square mile on average. The highway to Thermopolis passes through eons of geologic history an arms-length away.

After Yellowstone, the highway heads south then west through Goodale's Cutoff of the Oregon Trail. The settlers who took this cutoff found themselves in a bazar landscape of volcanic rock that tore their wagons apart. Here in Idaho atomic energy is mixed with antelope and cattle.

Bosie, Idaho, was nearly abandoned until gold was discovered. The Oregon Trail and the highway diverge after crossing the Snake then the Malhaur Rivers. Western Oregon is losing population until the highway reaches the Cascade Range. The counties there show some of the most rapid growth in the United States due, in part, to tourism and retirement communities. Then it's on to the Pacific Ocean and the fishing fleet at Newport

This corridor along U.S. 20 used the new form of transportation – the railroad – for western expansion rather than the wagons of the Overland Trail. It took only 20 years from the end of the Mexican war (1848), and only four years after the Civil War, before rails spanned the continent. While Chinese were used for the grueling work across the Sierra Nevada for the Central Pacific, the "Casement Army" of Irish ex-Civil War soldiers pushed the Union Pacific west. Former Union General Jack Casement drove his "army" forward laying four lengths of track per minute.

Other lines soon made a web of transportation. Small, short lines were built, bought, merged, became bankrupt, and merged again. The railroads advertized with provocative incentives for homesteaders to travel their lines to new land. New towns sprang up along the tracks. Soon cattle were taking the reverse route back east.

The history of the railroads in western migration is not complete without mention of the Orphan Trains. From 1854 to 1929, trains carrying babies, children, and youth left the east, primarily from New York City, for the west. During the intervening years an estimated 100,000 to 150,000 children were placed for adoption with families in 47 states. By 1910, the Children's Aid Society of New York had placed more than nine thousand in Illinois, 6,675 in Iowa, 3,442 in Nebraska, 19 in Wyoming, 52 in Idaho, and 90 in Oregon. Descendants of these children get in touch with others having the same origins by using the World Wide Web.

The disparity in numbers attributed to each state may be because the Northwestern Railroad did not reach Wyoming until 1886, although the Union Pacific did get there much sooner. A total of 68 separate lines, mainly for mining, existed in Wyoming at one time or another. A spur from the Union Pacific did not get to Idaho until 1874.

Who were these mountain men, military explorers, emigrants, cattlemen and soldiers who opened up this virgin land (from the white man's perspective)? Most passed on to other adventures. A few stayed to embellish this corridor with their English, Irish, German and Swedish names. Nevertheless, one cannot complete the history of this corridor without recognizing the Native American names. I will integrate the history of the Indian Wars along this corridor into this narrative of "manifest destiny."

CHAPTER ONE:
ILLINOIS (1818)*

"This declared indifference, but, as I must think, covert real zeal for the spread of slavery, I cannot but hate. I hate it because of the monstrous injustice of slavery itself. I hate it because it deprives our republican example of its just influence in the world-enables the enemies of free institutions, with plausibility, to taunt us as hypocrites – causes the real friends of freedom to doubt our sincerity, and especially because it forces so many really good men amongst ourselves into an open war with the very fundamental principles of civil liberty-criticizing the Declaration of Independence, and insisting that there is no right principle of action but self-interest." Lincoln's response to Douglas' Freeport Doctrine 1858

This journey of discovery of the roots of the settlement across the prairies begins in Rockford. U.S. 20 follows the sound of wagon wheels, stage coach wheels and iron wheels and the sound of the English, German, Swedish, and Irish voices of those who were the first travelers and settlers along the future route of the highway.

While the westward traveler begins the trek on U.S. 20 at Rockford, the history of this section in Illinois begins in Galena, nearly across the state. Galena (called La Pointe at the time, 1814) was the first white settlement in Illinois. Lead brought the miners from points south up the Mississippi River to the Galena River (originally the Fever River). The ore was removed in the opposite direction.

The Winnebago Treaty of 1829 at Prairie du Chien annexed land in Wisconsin and Illinois in return for payment (See the Black Hawk War below). The same year President John Quincy Adams opened the mouth of the Rock River to settlements.

In 1825, Oliver W. Kellogg headed for Galena from Peoria with a wagon following Indian Trails. He crossed the Rock River near the present Dixon heading northwest eventually establishing some cabins at Kellogg's Grove in Stephenson County. His trail became the first land route to Galena.

*The Year of Statehood Is Listed for Each State

ROCKFORD, WINNEBAGO COUNTY

county 514 mi^2, population 542/mi^2

In spite of its location on a mud flat, by 1833 Chicago was becoming a commercial center. The route of the ore wagons from Galena was shorter to Chicago, about 80 miles. They had to cross the Rock River and the future site of Rockford was chosen.

The history of Rockford is a good example of the western expansion along what would become U.S. 20. In 1833, Germanicus Kent, with his family and Negro slave, Lewis Lemon, arrived in Galena where Kent's brother, Aratus Kent, was a Presbyterian minister. The minister advised his brother of the bounty of the land east of Galena on the Rock River. The next year Kent settled on the west side of the Rock River and build a sawmill. In 1835, Daniel Shaw Hight, his wife and her sister, and others, settled on the east side. The same year, Dr. J.C. Goodhue selected the obvious name for the town, Rockford. Kent established a ferry. At the town's first election, comprising all of 120 votes, the following were elected: *William L. May, for member of Congress; John Turner, for representative to the State Legislature; Daniel S. Haight, for sheriff; Eliphalet Gregory, for coroner; Thomas B. Talcott, Simon P. Doty, and William E. Dunbar, for county commissioners; D.A. Spaulding, for county surveyor, and Daniel M. Whitney, for county recorder.* These names indicate the decidedly English origins of the first settlers. Lewis Lemon eventually bought his freedom for $800.

On January 1, 1838, the first stage coach arrived in Rockford. Six years later a bridge over the Rock River was constructed. By 1850, the population was 2,563 and two years later the city of Rockford was established. The first mayor was Willard Wheeler. The same year the first train of the Galena and Chicago Union Railroad arrived. Soon after, a train of Swedish immigrants stopped at the end of the tracks. The visit was caused by a cholera epidemic in Chicago. The conductor was told to get as far away as the track would carry him. The Swedes stayed and contributed immeasurably to the prosperity of the city. Nevertheless, two years after the Swedes arrived cholera visited the city.

Only a year later, cholera did not keep Attorney Abraham Lincoln from representing John H. Manny in his patent suit against Cyrus H. McCormick. Manny won.

The city was becoming an industrial site as can be seen by the factories along the river today. This industry brought in new emigrants. By the 1900 census, there were 31,051 inhabitants including 6,204 Swedes and 212 Blacks. Today in Winnebago County, 22% claim German ancestry, 11% Irish, 11% African-American and 8% English.

Those who remember the film *A League of their Own* may recall that one of the women's teams was the Rockford Peaches, 1942-43.

If one plans to begin this trip in Rockford, Illinois, this traveler recommends using the 20 Bypass to avoid a long ride on Business 20 down the urban sprawl along State Street to the city proper. Exit the bypass at state road 2 north. It will take you directly into town and to many of the sites worth visiting. There are so many attractions that this traveler suggests going to the web site to plan the visit. The river is lined with brick factories and the Riverfront Museum Park And Discovery Center, and the Rockford Art Museum. The unique Anderson Japanese Garden and the Tinker Swiss Cottage are a bit further but worth a visit. The Swiss Cottage is much more than a cottage. Built in 1865, it contains an elegant representation of the furnishings of the era. There is a trolley station with a functioning trolley on the east side of the river.

Leaving Rockford on 20 heading for Freeport, the road crosses from Winnebago County to Stephenson County named after Colonel Benjamin Stephenson who served in the War of 1812, in the Illinois militia during the Black Hawk War, and in the U.S. Congress.

FREEPORT, STEPHENSON COUNTY

564 mi^2, population 86/mi^2

The land between Rockford and Freeport is farm country. "In 1827, German settlers from Pennsylvania began arriving in the Freeport area to make their homes. Among them was William 'Tutty' Baker, who is credited as the founder of Freeport, and who built a trading post on the banks of the Pecatonica River. A generous man, Tutty Baker began operating a free ferry across the river and even invited travelers into his home for meals and lodging." (From the history of Rockport) Originally called Winneshiek; the community took its name from the fact of Baker's renowned generosity – "Free Port" – when it incorporated. Winneshiek was later dropped but is preserved to this day by the

Freeport community theater group. Each August, Freeport remembers Tutty Baker with a joyous festival. It became known as the Pretzel City USA when Billerbeck Baker flooded the city with pretzels in 1869.

Freeport became a city and railway center and the county-seat of Stephenson County in 1838. Linked by stagecoach with Chicago, the community grew rapidly. In 1840, a frame courthouse was erected and the first school was founded. Within two years, Freeport had two newspapers and in 1853 the two were joined by a third which published in German.

By then, the community had a population of 2,000.

"On August 27, 1858, the most significant of the historic Lincoln-Douglas debates took place in Freeport and gave the nation direction in succeeding years. Although Douglas won the election and retained his senate seat, his reply to a question on slavery alienated the South, which called it the 'Freeport Heresy,' and split the Democratic Party. This enabled Lincoln to win the presidency in 1860." A statue commemorating the debate sits in the city's center.

In 1901, the Historical Encyclopedia of Illinois described Freeport: "[H]as good water-power from the Pecatonica River, with several manufacturing establishments, the output including carriages, wagon-wheels, wind-mills, coffee-mills, organs, piano-stools, leather, mineral paint, foundry products, chicken incubators and vinegar. The Illinois Central Railroad has shops here and the city has a Government postoffice building." Population in 1890 was 10,189; in 1900 - 13,258.

LENA

After leaving Rockford and passing through Freeport and Elroy, look for the sign on the right for the Stage Coach Trail leading to Lena. There is some question where the town's name originated, but there is no question it is worth a side trip. (Maybe being about half way to Galena, it's just Lena.)

The magnet for children (and boys of all ages) is the C.W. & Lena R.R., M.N. Polhill, president. The G gage model rail road swings through a miniature town and countryside bordered by a flower garden. Upon entering the town, turn left on Schuyller St., cross the R.R. tracks (for big trains) and stop at the Tourist Information Center and gift shop. Mrs. Polhill runs the shop and Mr. Polhill runs the train next door. Since the last visit Mr. Polhill finds getting around more difficult so let Mrs. Pohill you want to see the trains. Mr. Polhill's grandfather took part in building U.S. 20 nearby using his horses.

A RV park is available between the first and second exits (Il. 53) to Lena.

Lena also boasts an Opera House built in 1878, a historical museum, a cheese factory, the Stagecoach Inn (1848), a State Park for camping, a golf course and a bed and breakfast.

The history of this little town mirrors the settling of the area and is well documented in *A Walk Through History: Lena and the Surrounding Area* by Margaret E. Scholtz.

Lena's history really begins with the lead mines of Galena as did Rockford's. Until Oliver Kellogg hacked out a trail to Galena in 1826-27, the miners had to take the Mississippi River up to the Galena River. The Kellogg Trail allowed the miners from Indiana, Kentucky and southern Illinois to arrive in the spring and leave before winter set in.

Then the Fink and Walker Stage Company acquired the U.S. Mail route from Chicago to Galena traveling part of the Kellogg Trail.

John Garner arrived with his family from Kentucky in 1834 and soon wrote his son-in-law Samuel Dodds to come on. Dodds arrived in 1837 and built the Buck Horn Tavern which soon turned into an inn along the stage route. Soon a finer inn was built with a distinguished list of visitors: Stephen A. Douglas, Horace Greeley, Jefferson Davis and maybe Grant and Lincoln. When a post office was needed, Dodds named the village Aida but it was changed to Taira Haute when Albedo, a town several miles away kept getting Aida's mail. The McEathron General Store sprang up. A town was in the making. The first school house was built in 1849.

Then the Galena and Chicago Union Railroad – which became the Illinois Central Railroad – followed the stage line through town in 1854 ending the stage era. As the story goes one of the railroad officers named the town after his daughter, Lena, and the name stuck. The railroad brought an influx of new settlers including an interesting Baptist preacher, J. E. Ambrose. He was an inventor of a railroad lamp and a conductor on the underground railroad to Canada.

In 1868, Lena had three medical doctors.

The town of Lena was incorporated in 1866 and boasted a population of 1,500. The list of businesses and their owners presents a snapshot of the settlement: The newspaper, the *Lena Star*, was started in 1867 by John W. Gishwiller with Samuel Dodds as the editor. It was finally owned by S.J. (Bossley) Schildhammer. A cigar factory started by Mick Simmons was taken over by "Pappy" Wingart. The cooper shop was owned by Henry Valkman and H. S. Diesdtlemeir owned the harness shop.. A slaughter house using ice cut from the river kept hogs frozen for shipment to Chicago. According to the 1880 census Lena had a bank (1867), hotel, opera house built by F.E. Beine, a flower mill, two grain elevators, seven churches, a wagon factory, six blacksmiths and 40 stores for sundries.

When the Chicago Great Western railroad came through Pearl City, Kent and Stockton south of Lena, it decreased the importance of Lena as a farming and manufacturing center.

The stage route went through Eleroy, present population 63, before arriving in Lena. A group of Germans all the way from Lippe Detmold in northwestern Germany settled the area in 1837.

After Lena, the line went through Waddams Grove. In 1832, William Wadams [sic] a miner from New York State traveled east from Galena. He found a limestone ridge where he built a cabin and called the site West Point. When the railroad came through the little town was moved down the hill and renamed "Waldheim Grove." Human Montague from Massachusetts settled in 1865 with nursery stock. Baptist, Methodist, Brethren and Dunker Churches sprang up as soon as a village was set down.

Just across the county line in Jo Daviess County sits what is left of Nora on the stage and railroad route. Garret Garner settled there in 1846. In 1872 it had 1,046 in habitants about 10 times what it has today. German settlers came looking for lead to mine but found the land excellent for farming instead. Soon a large tobacco industry sprang up.

Farther along the stage route, the town of Warren can brag about having the first woman mayor in Illinois and the second in the nation. This took place in 1915 before the passage of women's suffrage. Apparently, she was quite feisty and decided not to run for a second term. The town was established in 1834 by Kingsky Olds Sr. and Thomas Hicks from England. The town was named for Warren Burnett. Cholera appeared to follow along the western expansion and in 1854, it visited Warren where more than 50 people died of the disease.

Continuing on the stage and railroad route, the Apple River Canyon State Park marks the site where Millville once stood. In 1828, a fellow known only as Kirker built a cabin, but it was never occupied until after the Black Hawk war. A grist mill was built and the town flourished, adding a post office in 1838. A flood caused by heavy rains and a ruptured dam sent the whole town down the river in 1892. Earlier, 52 town-people died of cholera.

There are a couple of towns off the stage and railroad line that are interesting. North of Lena, the Pecatonica River gave Lyman Brewster from Peru, Illinois, a site to settle down in 1833. There the town of Winslow grew up. John Bradford and Thomas Loring were invited to come from Plymptom, Massachusetts, to build a sawmill. At that time, the material had to come by rail to Pittsburgh, by steamboat down the Ohio River and up the Mississippi to the Galena River and by wagon along the Kellogg Trail to

Winslow. By 1887, the Freeport, Dodgeville and Northern railroad line passed through town.

The town of Kent was established in 1835. Apparently, in 1832, there was a skirmish with Black Hawk near by. James Timms, Harris Giddings, Gilbert Osborn were some of the early settlers. The town may have been named after the circuit rider Aratus Kent (see Rockford). When the Chicago and Northwestern railroad came through, the town was moved to straddle the railroad.

In 1919, a road from Freeport to Dubuque was planned and two routes were proposed. One called the Grant Highway north of Lena and one called the Atlantic Yellowstone and Pacific Trail (AYP) passing through Lena. The AYP Trail route was chosen. At the time, when finished in 1923 it was called route 5 and eventually became U.S. 20, the Yellowstone Highway.

Up until the Federal Aid Highway Act of 1916, road building was at the whim of the states and local politicians. One wag commented, "The highways of America are built chiefly of politics, whereas the proper material is crushed rock or concrete."

According to the 2000 census, Stephenson County ancestries were German 45.7 %; Irish 12.3 %; English 11.2 %; Dutch 6.7 %; and Swedish 2.5 %; with 7.0 % listed as "U.S." The U.S. corresponds to the present 7.7 % Back listed by race.

THE BLACK HAWK WAR

The settlement of this area was strongly influenced by the presence of Indians and the Black Hawk War. As can be seen by the dates for the founding of the towns along this route, the opening up of the area to settlers depended on the outcome of the war. The best documented account can be found in Allen W. Eckert"s *Twilight of Empire*. He observes in the Author's Note: "Step by step, this series (of books devoted to the subject of western expansion) moves across the continent, showing clearly and in most fundamental terms how the land was won – through encroachment, trickery, warfare, deceit, treachery, purchase, alliance, gift, theft, and treaty." Names of significant players in this drama will be familiar to the reader.

When he was 13 years old in 1780, Black Hawk watched the Revolutionary hero, George Rogers Clark, burn his village (as mentioned in volume one). At this time, many of the tribes were fighting for the British along the Ohio frontier and Black Hawk joined the fighting during the War of 1812. Later, the Sac village, Saukenuk, was located on the Rock River near where it enters the Mississippi. Farther north, the Indians had mined the hills around Dubuque for lead before the white incursion.

In 1804, William Henry Harrison (future president), as territorial representative, bought the Illinois land in a shady deal that tricked the Indian signers who had no idea what they were giving away. The same year a small party of Sacs, including the wife of the spokesman, approached a cabin in Missouri to ask that they live peacefully. The white leader bludgeoned the spokesman with his rifle, threw the woman down, and attempted to rape her while the other white men held their rifles on the Indians. The spokesman recovered and buried his tomahawk in the man's head. The upshot was three dead white men and a demand that the Indians be caught and punished.

White squatters continued to arrive in Indian lands, some egged on by Henry Dodge who will be a central figure in the Black Hawk War and encroachment of Indian lands farther west. With the opening of the Erie Canal to the Great Lakes, emigrants from the east could travel to Chicago by water. These incursions around Galena in 1827 provoked a young Winnebago Chief Red Bird to declare war which Black Hawk joined. After some isolated attacks (hardly a war), it was agreed that the Sacs should live across the Mississippi in Iowa. President Andrew Jackson (of Trail of Tears fame) put the Sac land up for white purchase under the Indian Removal Act of 1830. George Davinport purchased more than 2000 acres including the Saukenuk region. In1832, Saukenuk was destroyed and the Indian graves vandalized. Black Hawk sent emissaries to the British expecting help which was refused. During this time there were also instances where tribe ambushed tribe.

On April 5, 1832, Black Hawk led about 350 warriors and more than 600 women and children across the Mississippi to the Rock River with intention of joining the Winnebago tribe. Gen. Henry Atkinson attempted to gingerly follow fearing that many more Indians were in the party. His attitude was "take no prisoners." A young Lt. Colonel Zachary Taylor (future president) was among the soldiers. Governor Reynolds called up the militia – all men between 18 and 45. Their pay would be 21 to 25 cents per day. Among them was a 23-year-old store clerk by the name of Abraham Lincoln. His colleagues elected him captain of his company.

By May 14, the band of Indians was cut off and starving and without the expected help of the Winnebago. Black Hawk decided to ask to return down the Rock River to Iowa. He camped near a group of militia lead by Major Isaiah Stillman. Under a white flag, three Indians approached the bivouacked militia while other scouts watched. The three Indians were surrounded by a bunch of drunken men and abused. The white flag carrier shouted, "Wait, we talk!" He was shot. The other two miraculously escaped among the drunken mob while other militia chased after the scouts. Black Hawk placed his warriors in formation and then charged the undisciplined mob of militia following the scouts. The militia panicked and ran and the whole camp disintegrated into fleeing men leaving all their supplies, equipment, food, and ammunition which the Indians found quite useful.

Up to this moment there had been no bloodshed. The Battle of Stillman's Run angered the Indians and gave them courage to believe that they could now sue for peace. By May 18, Black Hawk's band had permanent camp on the Pecatonica River in Wisconsin and was sending out war parties. The Winnebago and Potawatomies emboldened by the battle sent out their own war parties. The militia was mustered out but Lincoln rejoined. The area from Galena to Chicago, from Peoria north into Wisconsin was terrorized. Surviving settlers "forted up."

For the next two months, minor skirmishes and isolated massacres of settlers occurred. Col. Henry Dodge, commanding the Michigan Militia, led a skirmish on the Pecatonica River in Illinois. On June 24, the Apple River Fort was attacked resulting in three dead settlers and no Indian deaths. The village around the fort was pillaged. The next day a much more substantial battle was fought at the remains of Kellogg's Grove. The embattled soldiers were saved by the arrival of the calvary.

By July 10, Black Hawk's band had disappeared. Acting on Indian information, General James Henry and Colonel Dodge cut Black Hawk's trail as he headed for the Mississippi River in Wisconsin. At the Battle of Wisconsin Heights, June 16, Black Hawk preserved most of his ragged band. One chief tried to contact the pursuing troops to ask for safe passage to Iowa but was ignored. Some of his band were sent down the Wisconsin river only to be massacred near Prairie du Chien.

The pursuing troops were too worn out to follow but a whole new contingent of army and militia caught the depleted band trying to cross the Mississippi at Bad Axe Creek, August 1. A white flag carried by Black Hawk was considered a trap by a young lieutenant on the steam ship *Warrior* and the assembled Indians were massacred by canon grape shot and rifle fire. The troops came upon the remaining Indians on August 2. Between them and the *Warrior* most of the remaining Indians were killed. Those who happened to escape to the Iowa side were killed or captured by Sioux.

Black Hawk hid in Wisconsin until discovered in Wisconsin Dells and brought into Prairie du Chien August 27. There he was turned over to Colonel Zachary Taylor who sent him down to Galena and then Jefferson Barracks near St. Louis under a guard commanded by Jefferson Davis (the same). First, dragging around a ball and chain, Black Hawk and a few other chiefs were sent to Washington where he spoke with President Jackson. Then he was sent on a tour of the major cities of the east to impress him of the weight of the U.S. presence. Duly impressed, he vowed never to go to war again, and returned to the Sac reservation where he died in 1838.

As a side note to this war that didn't have to happen, President Jackson ordered Gen. Winfield Scott (hero of the Mexican War, 1846. See volume one.) to assume command of the war effort. Scott was to take eight hundred U.S. Army officers and soldiers west via the Great Lakes to Chicago. Additional troops would travel by steamboat up the Mississippi to meet him. Ultimately, Scott and his soldiers never reached the fighting. "On the way to Chicago, his troops were exposed to the cholera epidemic that swept the United States that year (killing many times more people than the Black Hawk War). By the time they reached Chicago on July 10, less than a quarter of the men remained healthy and they had to be quarantined." Of his command, 190 died and 180 deserted.

Scott, after treating some of his soldiers himself, reached Galena the day after the massacre at Bad Axe Creek. He went on to Rock Island where cholera caught up again.

Cholera, as we have seen, was a frequent visitor among the emigrants whether on the Overland Trail or in settlement towns. Although the possibility of contagious diseases had been hypothesized for centuries, it wasn't until 1854 that John Snow demonstrated that cholera was water born. Pasteur showed the existence of bacteria in the next decade. It wasn't until 1883 that the causative organism, *Vibrio cholerae*, was isolated. One can't ignore the bacterial infection today. The *New York Times* reported in August, 2005, that there were 24,621 reported cases in West Africa that year with 401 deaths. More recently it has decimated Zimbabwe.

The Black Hawk War really opened up the country to emigration. Not only did soldiers return to Illinois but also the news of the day gave others ideas of new land to explore. Eckert estimates a total of 250 whites lost their lives. Many more Indians died, and all those remaining in the area from southern Wisconsin to southern Illinois had to move west.

THE APPLE RIVER FORT

After following the Stage Coach Trail through Nora, this traveler headed back to 20 and Stockton on SR 78. In Elizabeth, the Apple River Fort is an excellent source of history. Entering from the east, look for the museum parking lot on the right at Myrtle Street. The fort is a replica of one hastily thrown up during the Black Hawk War. The museum is a gem of historical information including a video re enactment of the war itself sensitive to the harsh treatment of Indians. The city derives its name from the three Elizabeths who helped defend the fort during the Indian attack.

Across from the museum is the old R.R. depot: The Chicago Great Western Museum.

GALENA, JO DAVIESS COUNTY

county 601 mi^2, population 37/mi^2

After Stockton, the land turns hilly, the trail running along Terrapin Ridge looking down on farm country on each side. It is a single lane road, with few passing zones, the site of many accidents as the tourists from Chicago "make time."

The traveler has already learned something of the early history of Galena as a lead mining town. In the 1840s, Galena was producing 70% of the world's lead according to an Illinois history. Some 15,000 people lived here during the Civil War. The town filled "with bankers, merchants, and speculators who built mansions, hotels, and emporiums studded with the fine goods and furnishings from around the world." The California gold rush, played-out mines, a river silting up from mine-induced erosion and a national economic panic all drove Galena to become a handsome ghost town. Beginning in the 1960s, the town was rejuvenated for tourists – particularly those from Chicago –

preserving the 1860s atmosphere. The present population is less than 4,000. After spending at least a half-day in Rockford and visiting Lena and Elizabeth, plan for a day's stay in Galena by making room reservations in advance. After years of decay, Galena has renewed itself as a tourist destination and, thus, an easy trip from Chicago. As you enter the town, look for Frank O' Dowd's Irish Pub, stop at the Irish Cottage a reasonable place to stay. Young women dance on weekends. Children as well adults will enjoy the Irish dancing of four young girls reminiscent of Riverdance.

U.S. Grant's home is the first opportunity for a stop after checking out the pub. Children will wonder how meals were made on the wood-burning cook-stoves of the time. Galena boasts the origins of nine Civil War generals one of whom was a full-blooded Seneca on Grant's staff, Eli. S. Parker. He wrote the conditions of surrender at Appomattox.

U.S. GRANT

At the battle of Chapultepec, a young Second Lieutenant, Ulysses S. Grant, captured the attention of several superior officers, including Robert. E. Lee, by using a small howitzer stationed on a church belfry to scatter the Mexican soldiers. He was promoted to captain for this exploit. After the war he found military life isolating and boring. When he resigned his army commission, he found farming not productive and, migrating to Galena, store-keeping even less so. When the Civil War started he was appointed in charge of an Illinois militia regiment by Gen. John Charles Fremont (see chapter seven). Later, he was re commissioned as a Brigadier General. His victories at Forts Henry and Donaldson and rescuing the Union army at Shiloh brought him to Vicksburg and its final surrender opening up the Mississippi and strangling the Confederacy. The rest is history. After the war he returned to Galena and in 1868 went on the campaign trail for president. He returned to Galena to learn of his victory by telegraph..

EXPLORING GALENA

Continuing down the street from the Grant house, the railroad depot is the next must stop because it is the Visitor Center. For any serious stay in Galena you can't get along without its maps and recommendations unless you already have the Visitors Planning Guide.

It will soon become clear that Galena is in the bottom of a bowl of hills bisected by the Galena River. The quaint stores along S. Main St. are protected from flooding by a levee and a huge gate closing up Main Street. Before the wagon road followed by the stage coaches to Chicago, the lead ore (lead sulfide, L. *galena*) was carried down the river to the Mississippi. Galena was populated during the lead mining rush by lead miners from Missouri, followed by emigrants from Chicago, Irish and Germans.

Just a few of the many attractions in town are the Washburne House State Historic Site (where Grant learned that he had been elected president), the old customhouse (it remains the Galena Post Office), an old blacksmith shop, market house, and stockade. The Desoto House Hotel and Courtyard Restaurant is worth a look-in if not dining-in. The Galena/Jo Daviess County Historical Society and Museum, located in a 1858 mansion one steep block above Main Street, is worth the tour for the history and landform model of the town's location.

There is a sufficient list of eating establishments to satisfy any taste. There are several golf courses as well as skiing nearby and a winery for tasting. You may have noticed the entrance to Galena Territory on your way into town. Besides golf courses and a resort/spa, the area boasts about 1,900 homes, most of them summer getaways.

Jo Daviess County itself was organized in 1827, and was bounded as follows: Beginning on the Mississippi River at the northwestern corner of the state, thence down the Mississippi to the north line of the Military Tract, thence east to the Illinois River, thence north to the northern boundary of the state, thence west to the place of beginning. Galena was named as the county seat. Eventually, Winnebago and Stephenson Counties as well as six others were carved out of this huge tract of land.

The flavor of the origins of the first settlers can be tasted in the following document:

Among those who have been prominent in the history of this county, who arrived in 1827, are, Dr. Horatio Newhall, Capt. H. H. Gear and family, John G. Hughlett, James G. Soulard, William B. Green, Harvey Mann, Charles Peck, Solomon Oliver, Allan Tomlin, Gov. Thomas Ford, Col. James M. Strode, C.C.P. Hunt, Capt. John Atchison, Paul M. Gratiot, Nathaniel Morris, Moses Hallett, Lucius H. and Edward Langworthy, William Hempstead, D. B. Morehouse, and many others whose names are familiar in Jo Daviess County. (Excerpt taken from History of Jo Daviess County - 1878 by H. F. Kett & Co.)

The first explorer was Le Seuer, who reported the discovery of lead in 1700. Another Frenchman (Bouthillier) was the first permanent white settler, locating on the site of the present city of Galena in 1820. In 1827, county organization was effected, the county being named in honor of Gen. Joseph Hamilton Daviess, who was killed in the Battle of Tippecanoe. The name Galena was given to the county-seat (originally Fredericks' Point) by Lieutenant Thomas, Government Surveyor, in 1827. (*Historical Encyclopedia of Illinois,* Newton Bateman, editor, 1901.)

CHAPTER TWO:
IOWA (1846)

John Kinsella"Is this heaven?"
Ray Kinsella"It's Iowa."
John"I could have sworn it was heaven."
Field of Dreams

On your way west out of Galena, don't forget to take a short side-trip up SR 64 to the Vinegar Hill Lead Mine and Museum (but check with the visitor center first to see if it is open). This area where the corners of Illinois and Wisconsin meet Iowa is called *driftless* because the glaciers never deposited their burden. It is bedrock around Galena and Dubuque.

Passing over the Mississippi at Dubuque Iowa, this traveler found the river full of small boats and the river front full of visitors for the river festival and bass fishing championship. The National Mississippi River Museum and Aquarium are part of the river front. The "Treaty House" where Winfield Scott signed the treaty to end the Black Hawk war is also in the town.

Climbing out of Dubuque, 20 becomes a four-lane highway. Soon the twin spires of the Dyersville Basilica of St. Francis Xavier can be seen from the highway. They lead the traveler to the town proper up highway 136. When you leave 20, look for the National Farm Toy Museum at the intersection. It represents a miniature history of farming never to be seen again.

DYERSVILLE, DUBUQUE COUNTY

608 mi^2, population 147/mi^2

A few settlers, mostly English, were scattered about this vicinity in 1837. The first deed for land in the community was recorded by Joseph Hewitt on August 8, 1839. A group of Bavarians settled in the area in 1846. Covered wagons brought ten families comprising 42 emegrants. They homesteaded and became the nucleus of the farming community.

James Dyer arrived in the area in 1847, at the age of 26, and selected this site for his settlement. His family and friends followed from Somersetshire, England, in 1848 and a community was established. The town was known as Dyersville as early as February 13, 1849.

The financial panics and depressions of 1857 and 1873 caused many of the English to leave for places promising better fortunes in finance, commerce and trade, for which they had been trained. The English began to relinquish their leadership to the Germans with the arrival of the Bulingers, Forkenbrocks, Goerdts, Holschers and Schultzes.

The influx of Germans began when Bernard and Henry Holscher opened a General Merchandise Store on West Main in January of 1858. It was the first German speaking place of business. They started a trade center where farmers could buy their needs and sell their products. They attended church services at New Vienna for about 10 years. More and more German people settled here, and the place became a German Catholic settlement.

As the migration of the English out of the area continued, they sold farms, homes and stores to the Germans, who, by 1910. had taken an almost exclusive possession of Dyersville and the surrounding area. Many of the homes built by the early English still exist today. There are many descendants of the English living here also, some having married into German families. There is also a sprinkling of Irish, some of whose ancestors came with the building of the railroads and stayed.

"The cornerstone was laid for The Basilica of St. Francis Xavier June 3, 1888 by Bishop Hennessey of Dubuque. The church is of Gothic design, very impressive because of imposing size and height, and the two massive steeples, 200 feet high. It is large enough to accommodate 1,300 people. The facility was completely debt free by 1910, the result of 10 local German farmers putting their farms up for mortgage." (From the Dyersville web site)

"In 1947, the Cardinal Archbishop of Berlin, Germany, visited Dyersville, and was impressed by the stately church, which resembles some of the great churches in Europe. He was also impressed by the almost solid Catholic population of the surrounding territory. He remarked that it would be very fitting that this great church be raised to the dignity of a Basilica. Finally all the requirements were met and St. Francis Xavier Church was made a Basilica by His Holiness, Pope Pius XII, in 1956, after first having been solemnly consecrated in 1955. It was the 32nd Basilica named in the Untied States by 1956."

Breakfast at the Dyersville Family Restaurant gave us an opportunity to speak with the men's morning coffee club. Every small town has one. These men were retired farmers and a farm implement dealer. The country grows cattle feed and cattle. The land is flat with the strange mushrooms of silos poking up. The men reported that today many of the farms are owned by absentees.

Just 3.4 miles east of the town is the Field of Dreams Movie Site that welcomes visitors from 9am to 6pm. Continue through town on 136 to the sign for Field of Dreams to the right which will become Dyersville East Road.

RAMBLING

U.S. 20 is a divided four lane highway all the way to Fort Dodge. The more investigative traveler might want to try paralleling 20 on the blue highways. For example, we had lunch at the Princess Sweet Shop in Iowa Falls after passing through Reinbeck, Grundy Center, and turning north at Eldora to Pine Lake. The Princess is an authentic Art Deco soda fountain/restaurant of an era long gone from many cities. It is on the national register of historic places.

While eating lunch, I talked with a former farmer, John Roe. He confirmed that many of the farms had been bought by foreign companies and the farmers living on the farms got a portion of any profit. Several farm families also worked jobs in towns along the way. We drove through country that held huge complexes of what appeared to be poultry buildings with automatic feeding.

The side trips can take time away from more interesting visits. We tried to find some Amish crafts in the Amish country around Independence but finally seesawed on the country roads into and through Waterloo and on to Fort Dodge.

FORT DODGE, WEBSTER COUNTY

715 mi^2, population 56/mi^2

Our visit to The Fort Museum and Frontier Village, right off Business 20 in Fort Dodge made up for our wild goose chase earlier. Discovering life in the 19th century by searching in the general store, drug store, jail, livery was worth the effort. Then we toured the fort and its many rooms. There we met docent Don Smith who told us "more than you probably want to know" about one of the fort quartermasters in 1850, Lewis A. Armistead. He is the general who represents the high water mark of the Confederacy at Gettysburg dying in the breach in the Federal lines.

    The history of this fort is another example of the growth west pushing out the Indians. In 1835, Lt. Col. Stephan W. Kearny explored the area with the intention of finding sites for army outposts. Then, in 1850, a troop of soldiers returned the Sac and Fox Indians to their reservation in Kansas. They headed up the Des Moines River to establish a post "to protect settlers moving into Northwest Iowa." Note: these Indians had apparently been pushed out of their reservation in Iowa. Brevet Major Lewis A. Armistead had selected the site earlier. Named Fort Clark at first; it was renamed Fort Dodge for the U.S. Senator from Wisconsin Territory who, as founder of the 2nd U.S. Dragoons, was part of the group chasing Black Hawk. Rather than chasing Indians, chasing white trespassers off Sioux Indian lands, hunting down local bootleggers and pursuing deserters were the main occupations of the soldiers. The post itself existed only until 1853 and was then abandoned.

    The present fort is modeled after Fort Williams, built near the Minnesota border during the Civil War for protection against the Sioux uprising of 1862. The buildings along the main street and in the fort proper are originals brought in or reconstructed. The exhibit building is full of pioneer, military and Indian artifacts.

A visit to the Blanden Memorial Art Museum in town will uncover an eclectic collection of visual art. The docent was a from a family of long time residents. His grandfather had arrived as a blacksmith.

A written snapshot of emigrant life on the prairie is found in the letters of Gro Svendsen to her kin in Norway. The family settled in Emmet County north of Ft. Dodge in 1863. Immediately, Ole went to fight with Sherman and, upon returning, farmed the land through the 70s. The life wore Gro down and she died after the birth of her tenth child in 1878. The Svendsens were the vanguard of the 201,903 Iowa farmers listed in the 1890 census.

What attracted these farmers was the rich soil deposited by a series of glaciers reaching back tens of thousands of years and watered by rains above and aquifers below to nurture the prairie grasses with root systems reaching down as far as 23 feet. No wonder a breaking plow was invented to cut this underground forest which made-up the walls of the sod huts. In Iowa, prairie has been reduced from 30 million acres to 30,000, of which only 5,000 are formally protected.

THE SPIRIT LAKE MASSACRE

Spirit Lake, a settlement in the northwestern territory of Iowa near the Minnesota border, was comprised of settlers from Milford, Massachusetts. In mid March 1857, a small band led by local chieftain Inkpaduta (Scarlet Point) raided the settlement killing about 40 and abducting four women. Two were subsequently killed, one released voluntarily, and one ransomed. They were taken on a grueling journey through deep snow. A relief expedition sent from Ft. Dodge arrived only in time to bury the dead. Another, sent from Ft. Ridgely in Minnesota, pursued Inkpaduta, who fled westward, but failed to overtake him. The massacre was commemorated by a monument erected in 1895 at nearby Arnolds Park.

This was a minor uprising in protest of the 1851 Treaty of Traverse des Sioux. The massacre would be the first of a series of incidents leading up to the Sioux uprising in eastern Minnesota only five years later which was also in protest against the poor treatment by Indian Agents.

SIOUX CITY, WOODBURY COUNTY

119 mi^2, population 873/mi^2

U.S. 20 continues as a rather dangerous two lane road from the fort taking the traveler into the outskirts of Sioux City and I-29. The terrain gets hillier so that the corn fields are terraced. Coming over a rise, huge modern windmills appeared on the horizon slowly turning out their power, replacing the farm windmill that punctuated the landscape in earlier days.

A several hours stop at the Iowa Sergeant Floyd River Museum &Welcome Center (exit 149 on I-29) and the Lewis & Clark Interpretive Center is other highlight of this journey. The welcome center is a previously functioning river boat, the *Sergeant Floyd*, with three decks to investigate. Sergeant Charles Floyd was the only member of the Lewis & Clark expedition to die possibly of an intensional ailment. Visitors will be impressed by the amount of visual history packed into the ship.

Because the ship was launched in 1932 in Jeffersonville, Indiana, it had to come down the Ohio River to where it meets the Wabash River, then on to the Mississippi to St. Louis and the Missouri. The ship did river improvement work until 1983 when it was bought as surplus property by the City of Sioux City and dry-docked at its present site.

While you are at the welcome center, get a brochure *Nebraska Highway "20 (year)" To Adventure*. It will help with the next leg of the trip.

About the length of a football field from the welcome center, is the Lewis & Clark center, again packed full of sights and sounds. "The center focuses on a day in the life of the explorers as they traveled through what is now the Sioux City area. The death and burial of Sergeant Floyd on Aug. 20, 1804, is at the heart of the story. The expedition as a finely tuned military operation comes to life in exhibits that use dozens of interactive devices, including animatronic mannequins, the changing-river exhibit, map-making tools, computers, flip books, stamping stations, text-and-graphic panels, lift-and-drop panels, informational doors and drums, hand-painted murals, brass-rubbing stations, and replicas of military equipment and Indian artifacts. A videotape presentation, produced exclusively for the interpretive center, is shown every 15 minutes in the Keelboat Theatre." (From the brochure) And if you are lucky, a modern-day version of the explorer's canine companion will welcome you.

On the grounds is a garden containing many of the plants found along the Lewis & Clark route to Oregon and a garden containing Native American vegetables.

CHAPTER THREE:
NEBRASKA (1876)

"But a human tide, one that they could neither see nor hear, was rising in the east. It would be upon them soon. The good times of that summer were the last they would have. Their time was running out and would soon be gone forever."Dances With Wolves by Michael Blake

Leaving South Sioux City, the explorer finds the road turns into a two-lane "blue highway." A side trip south of 20 leads to the Winnebago Reservation where the tribe had been pushed further from Illinois and Iowa. The Indians hold their Pow Wow there in late August.

The Great Plains begins in earnest with farm homes less frequent and large expanses of land. This stretch across Nebraska parallels the Cowboy Trail following the old railroad right of way from the Iowa border to Wyoming (nearly 400 miles). Large cattle feedlots eventually give way to large ranges spotted with cattle. When this traveler came through, young, resting calves could be seen scattered like periods marking the landscape.

Using "Nebraska Highway '2005' To Adventure" this traveler found a description of every town along the route. Nearly each one appeared to have its museum and historical society. What is waiting the rambler is some wild goose chases, some disappointments, and eventually a snapshot of the settling of the West. While most of the emigrants headed up the North Platte River from Omaha, ranching expanded along the railroad.

Just a few miles inside of Nebraska on 20, state road 12 shoots off north 8 miles to the river town of Ponca. Nothing in the state guide for the town includes the sad history of the Ponca Tribe. The tribe's reservation is farther west where the Niobrara River meets the Missouri, at the town of Niobrara. Both towns are sites along the Lewis and Clark route.

THE PONCA

Quite a few miles west by northwest of the town of Ponca, Nebraska, is the Ponca reservation where several of the chiefs are buried. The reservation was established by treaty in 1858 to protect the tribe from other tribes and white incursions. These people, of Sioux origin, had been pushed by the tide of Indian displacement and white incursion into the Niobrara River valley.

They found an abundant land where they could grow crops and hunt until the incursions of the Pawnee and Lakota and the diseases of the white man constrained them. Similar to the Illinois situation, the treaty provisions never came; soldiers attacked a small group on their way to Omaha; and finally the Federal Government gave the reservation land to the Lakota. The Ponca was removed to Indian Territory (Oklahoma). A small band trekked back to their former land and the chiefs were arrested. The attitude of the local whites turned sympathetic and lawyers got them freed on writs of *habeas corpus*. This was the first time Indians were considered entitled to equal protection under the Constitution.

Through intermarriage and sale of individual allotments outside of the tribe, the Northern Ponca tribe slowly dissolved until Congress voted to "terminate" the tribe in 1961. Members became non-Indians losing their rights to government services. After years of litigation, the tribe was reinstated in 1990. They are also reestablishing their language, their identity – about two thousand members – and their powwows.

PLAINVIEW, PIERCE COUNTY

574 mi^2, population 14/mi^2

In 1880, the Nefrom & Norfolk railroad arrived in Plainview followed by the Pacific Short Line in 1890.The first stop of interest is the Old Johnson Hotel Café. We arrived just in time for lunch. It is partly restored and contains memorabilia of past eras. The hotel was built in 1901 and was once owned by Fred Astaire's grandfather where Fred and Astele were said to have played as children.

Sadly, the downtown itself is mostly boarded up. But there is a general store a few buildings from the café worth investigating. Emigrants arrived as early as 1873 from Wisconsin and Illinois, mainly Danish and German.

In 1879, Robert Louis Stevenson used the cross country railroad to visit his fiancee in San Francisco. He described Nebraska: "It was a world almost without a feature; an empty sky, an empty earth; front and back, the line of railway stretched from horizon to horizon, like a cue across a billiard-board; on either hand, the green plain ran till it touched the skirts of heaven." His assessment of the Nebraskan settler's view was compared to a civilized room: "His is a wall-paper with a vengeance–one quarter of the universe laid bare in all its gauntness. His eye must embrace at every glance the whole seeming concave of the visible world; it quails before so vast an outlook, it is tortured by distance; yet there is no rest or shelter, till the man runs into his cabin, and can repose his sight upon things near at hand."

ROYAL, ANTELOPE COUNTY

population 7,111, 8.7 per square mile

The county hit twice the present population between 1868 and 1883. One of the Mormon wagon trains crossed it coming up the Elkhorn River in 1846. The first permanent settler was Crandall Hopkins with his 12 children. He came from New York by way of Ohio, Wisconsin, Illinois and Iowa. By 1871, the best land had been taken mainly by settlers of English origin.

Zoo Nebraska, in Royal, advertises tigers, wolves, monkeys, and reptiles. The present population in Royal is 86 down from 250 in 1910. A couple of miles west of Royal the traveler is directed to turn right at the sign for the Ashfalls State Historical Park. Farther up the side road to Ashfalls is an opportunity to feast at Green Gables. The entrance to the park is 7 miles from 20. There is a minimal fee. *U.S.A. Today* listed this as "one of the 10 great places to soak up science."

This is a must-see for anyone, particularly families with children. The history of this paleontologic dig is well laid out. The Niobrara River valley area contains North America's most complete record of the 20-million year history of grassland animals. Ten million years ago, an enormous volcanic eruption in what is now southwestern Idaho sent a thick cloud of ash downwind into the central Great Plains. Herds of rhinos, camels, three-toed horses, and other animals around a water hole here were suffocated and eventually buried by blowing volcanic dust over a period of several weeks. Their perfectly preserved skeletons can be seen, lying in their death poses, now being uncovered in the "Rhino Barn" A very detailed interpretive center is worth spending a couple of hours in. Uncovered in 1953, the site is a Western animal Pompeii

O'Neill, HOLT COUNTY

County population 11,551, 48 persons per square mile, 99% white

Most of the way through Nebraska 20 parallels the railroad grade, often with the rails missing. As mentioned earlier, this right of way is being turned into the "Cowboy Trail" a hiking, biking and equestrian trail across the 321 miles of Nebraska. The last depot still existing along the route is located in O'Neill which announces itself, with some right, as "the Irish Capital of the U.S."

The first settlers in the immediate vicinity of O'Neill were H. H. McEvony, Frank Bitney, John T. Prouty, Eli Sanford, John Sanford and Eli H. Tomphson. They reached the Elkhorn about half a mile below the present site of O'Neill, July 13, 1873. In the succeeding autumn, Herman Hoxsie and his two sons, Wilson and Henry, David Wisegarver, Samuel Wolf, and some others located there.

In 1874, a sod house, 36 x18 feet, was the only home for 13 men, two women and five children until the crops were planted and logs dragged 18 miles to build cabins. The sod house was called "The Grand Central Hotel."

On the 12th of May 1874, Gen. John O'Neill, in honor of whom the town was named, arrived here with the first colony of his countrymen, consisting of Neill Brennan, Patrick S. Hughes, Timothy O'Connor, Henry Curry, Thomas Connolley, Michael H. McGrath, Thomas N. J. Hynes, Michael Dempsey, Thomas Kelly, Robert Alworth, Ralph Sullivan, Patrick Brennan, Thomas Cain, Henry Carey and Patrick McKarney.

Gen. John O'Neill, from County Monaghan, Ireland, was quite a character. Arriving in New Jersey, he tried several businesses before joining the Second Dragoons of Virginia in May 1857 under Colonel Albert Sidney Johnson and Lt. Colonel Robert E. Lee (both of Civil War fame). At the start of the Civil War he became a member of the first Cavalry and distinguished himself as a cavalry officer for the North. After the war he was part of the Fenian attempt to invade Canada in1870. Note: The Fenian Movement was named after legendary Irish warriors and it demanded Irish freedom from British rule. The invasion of Canada was intended to use the captured land as ransom for Irish freedom. President Grant refused to support the invasion. Captured, and imprisoned for a time, O'Neill moved into Nebraska and helped many of his Irish countrymen find land.

The flavor of the early settlement can be seen in the names: David Adams, banker; David Dark, county treasurer from Illinois; Ed Evans from New York by way of Wisconsin; Patrick Kahn, from County Mayo, New York, Wisconsin, and, finally, Lincoln, Nebraska. Kahn hired O'Neill to bring emigrants from the east; Patrick Haggard from Ireland; W.D.Mathews, editor of county newspaper from Stephenson County, Illinois; and John Agerter, stockman, directly from Switzerland in 1882.

At times, the little town was invaded by cowboys after they had been paid for their drives. They were expected to be rowdy as they spent their money. In one incident, a sherif of Holt County was killed by a cowboy. He was acquitted on a plea of self defense.

The traveler can pass quickly through Rock County named for its rocky soil. The population of 1,756 fills up the county, 1.74 persons per square mile. A 1890 list of farmers looks like the residents of an English village with a few Germans added. Brown County, population 3,503, with its major town Ainsworth, is also small and limited in population. The major religious institutions are Catholic, followed by Lutherans and Methodists.

VALENTINE -- CHERRY COUNTY

Cherry County is huge, 5,961 mi^2 but contains 6042 whites and 200 Indians or one person per mi^2.

Valentine becomes a canoeing center during the summer for visitors putting in on the Niobrara National Scenic River and a frequently used postmark around February 14.

The town grew out of the crew camp for the Sioux City & Pacific Railroad in 1883. At the time the area was still "unorganized territory" attached to Holt County. Fort Niobrara near by was established in 1879 to serve as a peace-keeping force for the Rosebud and Pine ridge Reservation Indians allowing white settlement in the area.

A paragraph in Valentine's history is fascinating: "The first election held in this area was in 1882 at the Deer Park Hotel across the river from the fort. Votes for Congressman E.K. Valentine had been highly solicited. Contractors were paid to transport the 300-or-so railroad workers to the polls so they could vote, which helped Valentine win the election. The settlement that developed was named 'Valentine' in his honor, and was chosen as the county seat for Cherry County." The history also honors the town's reputation of being the "toughest town in Nebraska." Pistol practice was common in the saloons.

MERRIMAN

The next town of any consequence is Merriman. Many small towns sprang up as the Fremont, Elkhorn & Missouri Valley Railroad was built across Nebraska. Note the railroad names keep changing as one line is purchased by others. One of these was a little cowtown called "Merriman," established in 1885 and named for the "rail-boss," James Merriman.

At one time all the ranchers in the area trailed their cattle to Merriman, making it the largest shipping point for cattle between Belle Fourche, South Dakota, and Omaha, Nebraska. It was a common sight to see the stockyards full of cattle and thousands still outside waiting for the train. The three-to-five-year-old long-horned steers were very wild. When the train whistled, the cattle often stampeded, tearing apart the stockyards as they went.

GORDON

The perceptive traveler may note that the rails end in O'Neill and began again in Merriman still following the Cowboy trail. The traveler will also notice the change in scenery as 20 enters the Sandhills area of the state. The Sandhills War (see below) was made famous by the novels of Mari Sandoz whose ranch is a few miles south of Gordon. There is a book store on Gordon's main street with her books as well as memorabilia. Her novel, *Cheyenne Autumn* was made into a film. North of Gordon is the Pine Ridge Reservation and the site of the Wounded Knee Massacre.

Another short side trip north from Valentine on highway 12 along the Niobrara River is the Fort Niobrara National Wildlife Refuge. Herds of buffalo, elk, and Texas longhorn cattle are present.

In the early 1870s, cattle ranches sprang up around the Niobrara River. The region to the south was considered uninhabitable sand hills. Then in the spring of 1879, the ranchers headed into this unknown territory trying to locate any cattle surviving the severe winter storms. They found their healthy cattle in well watered grasslands that became one of the most productive cattle-raising regions in the world.

As the "sod busters" filed claim on the government lands that the ranchers were using as open range, the ranchers were pushed out. But not without a fight called the

Sandhills War. Nevertheless open range ended in 1885 when the last round up was held, and the ranches moved west.

After Gordon, one can speed through small towns such as Clinton, Rushville and Hay Springs hardly noticing them. Nevertheless, these were important stops along the railroad. Today, Rushville is a declining town in a declining county, Sheridan. City population presently 926, it was the site where Buffalo Bill Cody gathered his wild west show. Its ancestry is, by rank, German, Native American, English and Irish with smaller percentages of Scandinavians and Hispanics. The massacre at Wounded Knee occurred just over the South Dakota boarder nearby.

WOUNDED KNEE

The northern part of Nebraska was Sioux country before the white invasion. The Sioux were initially friendly until the cow incident at Fort Laramie, Wyoming in 1854. Apparently, a cow owned by the Mormon wagon train passing though wandered away and was killed by an Indian whose camp was near the fort. The Mormons complained, but the cow had been eaten. The Mormons demanded arrest of the Indian. A 21-year-old lieutenant, John L. Grattan, was sent with 29 men and two cannons to get the Indian. The chief offered several ponies in payment but refused to turn the man over to the soldiers. The Lieutenant ordered his soldiers to fire the cannon and their rifles into the camp. The Indians retaliated by killing all of the soldiers. They then retreated north with the supplies stored for their use.

The next year all the Indians were told to live below the North Platte River. Anyone north would be considered hostile. Troops under the command of General W.S, "Whitebeard" Harney caught up with Little Thunder's group four miles north of the Platte on Blue Water Creek. According to some descriptions, Little Thunder tried to parlay but the soldiers started firing. The tribe scattered and they were individually massacred by the soldiers. As author Stephen R. Jones put it, "The blood would continue to flow for thirty-five years, at Fort Kearney, Rosebud Creek, Little Big Horn, and Wounded Knee."

The friendly Indians had turned enemies. After the Battle of the Little Big Horn, also known as Custer's Last Stand, 1876, the Sioux were finally put on the Rosebud reservation just north of Cherry County, Nebraska. Herds of cattle were trailed along the Niobrara River to feed the Indians.

In 1890, the Sioux became restless partly due to poor provisions. The U.S. Government sent soldiers to several towns in Cherry County to protect the settlers. The towns also formed militias. A large band of Indians, under Chief Big Foot, heading for Pine Ridge was halted by the Seventh Cavalry at Wounded Knee Creek about three miles north of Rushville. As the soldiers were attempting to take the rifles away, a shot rang out and the massacre began. Thirty-two soldiers and 150 Indians were killed. According to Mari Sandoz, George Armstrong Custer was the officer in charge. In leading the survivors back to an encampment, Custer chose an Indian maiden as his consort and had a son by her.

MUSEUM OF THE FUR TRADE

About 18 miles from Gordon, right before Chadron, the traveler will find another gem for the curious: the Museum of the Fur Trade. Here one can find the history necessary to understand the exploration of Wyoming and the rest of the West. The displays are extensive and quite informative. Scores of rifles of all descriptions chronicle the progression of firearm technology. The museum's three galleries discuss the fur trade from early colonial days to the present. The exhibits trace the everyday lives of British, French, and Spanish traders, voyagers, mountain men, professional buffalo hunters, and typical Plains and Woodland Indians. Exhibits include the entire range of trade goods, including munitions, cutlery, axes, firearms, textiles, costumes, paints, and beads. The actual site of the Bordeaux Trading Post is in the rear and makes clear the lifestyle of the time (1837-1876). The trading post, a sod and wood hut buried in the ground, and the warehouse were built along the Bordeauz Creek in 1833 and is surrounded by the only hilly, forested region in this part of Nebraska. The post was operated until 1876 when it was shut down after US soldiers confiscated ammunition being sold to the Indians.

CHADRON

In 1884 the Fremont, Elkhorn, & Missouri Valley Railroad pushed west from Valentine. The plan was to lay one line to Wyoming and a branch line north to the Black Hills. With knowledge of what the railroad was going to do, some enterprising people established a town at a point where Chadron Creek flows into the White River. The town's name is a misspelling of the man who ran a trading post, Louis Chartran.

A downward trend in the town's fate started with the Panic of 1893, and escalated because of a lack of rain causing crops to fail. To offset this, a 1,000 mile horse race from Chadron to Chicago was organized. While it created a great deal of interest all along the rail line, not much happened to stem the tide of bad times.

FORT ROBINSON STATE PARK

Half way between Chadron and the Wyoming border, Fort Robinson State Park is another signpost of history. The Fort Complex, containing officers and enlisted men's quarters, accommodations, areas for tent and RV camping, is a small part of a large park amenable to hiking and picnicking. It was an active military post from 1874 to 1948.

The post began in 1874 as a temporary cantonment during the turmoil of the frontier Indian Wars. It is the site where Chief Crazy Horse was assassinated.

Through the years, Fort Robinson was continually expanded and became one of the largest military installations on the northern plains. The post survived the frontier period and was used by the U.S. Army during World War II as a prisoner of war camp for Germans.

Originally named Camp Robinson, it was renamed for Lieutenant Levi Robinson who was killed in 1874 near Fort Laramie by Indians from the Red Cloud Agency while he was on a wood gathering detail. For the first four years, the post provided security for the nearby Red Cloud Agency. The soldiers also guarded the Sidney-Deadwood Trail to the Black Hills and the surrounding region. Although the agency was moved in 1877, Camp Robinson remained. As an indication of its permanent status, the designation "Camp" was changed to "Fort" in 1878.

The mid-1880s brought a critical change to the history of Fort Robinson. The Fremont, Elkhorn & Missouri Valley Railroad had arrived, and the army decided to expand the post. The railroad gave Fort Robinson a new strategic importance: Soldiers from the post could quickly be transported to trouble spots. In the late 1880s the fort was greatly enlarged and replaced Fort Laramie, Wyoming, as the most important military post in the region. The railroad guaranteed Fort Robinson's importance and prolonged its military occupation.

Another significant event in Fort Robinson's history occurred in 1885, when the first African American soldiers of the Ninth Cavalry ("Buffalo Soldiers") arrived. At that time the U.S. Army was totally segregated, with two cavalry regiments composed of black soldiers. From 1887 to 1898 the post was regimental headquarters for the Ninth Cavalry. From 1885 through 1907 the majority of the troops stationed at Fort Robinson were African American.

In the winter of 1890, attention turned to the Pine Ridge Indian Reservation with the Ghost Dance movement. The army was called in to monitor the volatile situation. The first soldiers sent to Pine Ridge were from Fort Robinson. Soldiers from the post were also sent to help quell several outbreaks of civil disorder during the miners' strikes of the 1890s.

CHEYENNE IMPRISONMENT

The Northern Cheyenne tribe had been removed from their traditional home to a reservation with their Southern Cheyenne kinsmen in Indian Territory (later Oklahoma) in 1877. The following year, after suffering from poor food and diseases and having been denied permission to return north, more than 350 Cheyennes[1] decided to break away from the reservation and head for the Yellowstone River 800 miles away.

Under the leadership of Chiefs Dull Knife and Little Wolf, the group moved northward through Kansas. Several clashes with army troops and civilians occurred, with the Indians each time able to elude recapture. Eventually, they were able to slip through a cordon along the Union Pacific rail line and the Platte River in Nebraska and resume their northerly trek.

Somewhere in Nebraska the group broke up. Little Wolf and his followers wanted to continue moving north and join the Lakota leader Sitting Bull in Canada. For the time being, they went into hiding in the vast Sandhills. The second group decided to try to obtain refuge with the Lakota chief Red Cloud, who was a friend of Dull Knife. With this in mind, they set out for the Red Cloud Agency. Unknown to Dull Knife, however, Red Cloud and his people had been moved into Dakota Territory, and only soldiers remained near the old agency.

South of present-day Chadron, Nebraska, an army patrol intercepted Dull Knife and his people, and on October 24, 1878, escorted them into Fort Robinson. A total of 149

---

[1] There is some question on the plural of Cheyenne. I will use Mari Sandoz's Cheyennes

men, women, and children were taken into custody and confined in the cavalry barracks. Initially the Cheyennes were free to leave the barracks as long as all were present for evening roll call. Several of the women were even employed at the fort, and this arrangement continued into December 1878.

By late December, they were prisoners in the barracks, no longer allowed to come and go. The army was under orders to pressure them into returning south, and the Cheyennes were equally determined never to go back to the southern reservation. By the night of January 9, 1879, the impasse had come to a point of crisis. They broke out of the barracks using weapons, they had hidden earlier, to shoot the guards, and while some of the men held off the soldiers, the remaining Cheyennes fled in the dark.

A running fight ensued along the White River valley. At least twenty-six Cheyenne warriors were killed that night and some eighty women and children were recaptured. Those still free eluded the soldiers until January 22, when most were killed or taken prisoner at a camp on Antelope Creek northwest of Fort Robinson. In all, sixty-four Native Americans and eleven soldiers lost their lives during the protracted escape attempt. Dull Knife and part of his family were among the few that managed to get away, and they eventually made their way to refuge with Red Cloud. This escape is the subject of the novel by Mari Sandoz and the film *Cheyenne Autumn*.

> *(Side Bar) Cheyenne Autumn* The film, the last of the John Ford westerns, is a poor attempt to describe the plight of these Native Americans. Still appearing on television, it adds unnecessary scenes with Jimmy Stewart as Wyatt Earp in Dodge City, Kansas. It ignores the valiant holdout by Little Wolf's band. I recommend the Sandoz book for a much better picture of this 1,500 mile long escape.

Little Wolf's band held out longer in the Sandhills. For three months the soldiers searched. The Cheyennes hunted elk, pronghorn, deer and gathered edibles. They survived minus 40 degree weather. After learning of the fate of Dull Knife's band, the hidden Indians headed toward the Yellowstone again. After several battles, they were caught 75 miles from their destination. The chiefs were imprisoned. Five years later the remnants of the tribe were settled on a reservation on the Tongue River in Montana.

CRAWFORD -- DAWES COUNTY

The traveler will note the change in topography from rolling hills to buttes with more pine trees. Dawes County population 8,457 white and 572 Native Americans to make 24/mi^2

The Red Cloud Buttes, named for Chief Red Cloud of the Teton Dakota Sioux, look down on Fort Robinson and, three miles northeast, on the town of Crawford, nestled along the White River. One can only imagine the rough and rowdy early history of soldiers, Indians, and cowboys ranging through the town.

In 1886, when Fort Robinson was twelve years old, the Fremont, Elkhorn, & Missouri Valley Railroad established stations at the fort and at a settlement soon to be known as "Crawford." A tent city immediately sprang up with every other establishment a saloon or gambling house. It is said that the man selling hardware piled the nail kegs inside the walls of his tent to keep stray bullets out.

A second railroad, the Chicago, Burlington, & Quincy, came through Crawford in 1889, when Nebraska's only railroad tunnel was completed through the Pine Ridge ten miles to the southeast. This spelled the demise of the Sidney to Deadwood Trail, route of the stage coaches and freight wagons to and from the gold mining towns in the Black Hills. Both rail lines now haul low sulfur coal from the Wyoming fields. The Crow Butte uranium deposit, discovered in 1981, is just south of Crawford

From Crawford to the Wyoming boarder, the land seems to flatten out again in preparation for the sage of the arid high plains country. On the way to Casper, U.S. 20

passes through the sparsely populated Sioux County, Nebraska, populated by 1440 whites and 2 Native Americans.

****

THE MYSTIC SANDHILLS

Let me pause here for a moment before we enter Wyoming and return to the Sandhills. U.S. 20 serves as the northern limit of the Sandhills. Covering about one-fourth of Nebraska, they reach 100 miles from the Niobrara River south to the Platte River and 200 miles east to west, three times the size of Massachusetts. To the casual traveler the treeless expanse appears desolate, foreboding.

The first traveler of written record, Scottish trapper James Mackay, described the land south of present Valentine as "a great desert of drifting sand without trees, soil, rocks, or animals of any kind, excepting some little varicolored turtles." His analysis was supported by several other explorers. The author of *The Last Prairie, a Sandhills Journal*, Stephen R. Jones, explains the differences in topography between these early impressions and the present conditions on the explorers' visits during the cycles of drought. Range management and fire suppression may have something to do with the greening of the Sandhills.

Jones observes that, "This is the largest area of grass-stabilized dunes in the Western Hemisphere." It is a huge wildlife refuge containing diverse ecosystems which he has well documented in his book. Along the Niobrara River, east meets and mingles with west: paper birch meet ponderosa pine, white tail deer meet mule deer. It's a heaven for bird watchers. Some 90 species can visit just one of the Sandhills lakes. The visitor can see eagles, several kinds of hawks and the pelicans outnumber the people.

Do not ignore the Sandhill cranes. These leftovers from the dinosaur era have been migrating from north of the Arctic Circle to the Gulf Coast for about three million years. They saw a different landscape of forests and swamps populated by the animals found at Ashfalls State Park: the camels, sabertooths, ground sloths and more. The Sandhills themselves are only 10 to 15 thousand years old. Will the sand cranes adapt to the melting of the arctic ice and the destruction of the river habitats such as the Platte? Thousands of visitors come to see their migration every year bringing in about $15 million a year to Grand Island, Nebraska, alone.

This was the home of the Pawnee, hunters and gatherers living along the river valleys. They planted their crops; hunted the abundant game and lived off a natural garden of edible plants. They were raided by the Sicangu (Brulé, Rosebud) and Oglala Lakota. It took 39 years from the first treaty with the whites in 1818 to the final sale of the land north of the Platte. In 1874, they too went to Oklahoma Territory. As historian George Bird Grinnell concluded, this was another example of "a carefully planned and successfully carried out conspiracy to rob (them) of their lands."

The influx of settlers was turned back by the wind, snow, heat, hail, grasshoppers and isolation. Many gave up and pulled out. Some went crazy. One housewife living near Rushville on Pine Creek hung herself from the rafters of her dugout. Stories persist of killer snows such as the "schoolchildren's storm of 1888." Some children made it home from school that day; some stayed until their building blew in. Some perished as the temperature bottomed out at minus 35. They didn't report wind chill back then.

An attempt to bring homesteaders in during the 1880s to plow the grassland ended in disappointment for all but the most hardy. An attempt at center-pivot irrigation during the 1960s and 1970s was minimally successful. From the advantage of air travel one can see these circles marching across the dry western land. Nevertheless, this is grass land not farm land.

Jones cites the example of Gideon and Margaret Waggoner from Indiana. In 1884, they left the train at Valentine and headed for Gordon with their farm animals and equipment. (Valentine acquired its name from the Vallintines of Texas who were part of the Waggoner party.) Margaret had four children; two died in infancy. They got by fairly well at first. Then the droughts of 1883-84-85 struck. Foreclosures became common. By 1899, nearly two-thirds of the homesteaders had left. The Waggoners quit but remained to work. The work-for-others enabled them to buy a small ranch. Margaret buried two husbands and two children before she died in Gordon in 1944.

No history of the Sandhills is complete without the Sandhills War. Cattle were grazed around Gordon and above the town, but not below. The Sandhills were considered useless until the blizzard of 1879. It blew the cattle south where they found grass and water in the valleys. This whole area is watered from the Ogallala aquifer below rather than the little rain that waters the farmers' hopes more than their crops.

As described earlier, the cowboys looking for the remnants of their herds found satisfied bovines in the Sandhills. Texas cowboy Jim Dahlman, when Mayor of Omaha, recalled: "We soon began to strike cattle, perfectly contented in their new home, amidst splendid grass and water in valleys, now the great hay meadows of the west . . . We rounded up this bunch of cattle and were certainly two surprised cowboys. Here were cattle as fat as any ever brought out of a feed lot; mavericks (un branded) from one to four years old. We could hardly believe our eyes." The era of the huge ranches began.

Bartlett Richards is the lighting rod for this history. At age 17, he left New England for the west for his health. He began as a cowhand in Wyoming. Soon he was investing his family's and friends' money in his own herd. At 20 he was running cattle for a group of British investors.

By 1888, he had consolidated into a huge ranch southeast of Chadron, the Spade ranch. He became the Chadron banker. The Spade ranch covered two thousand square miles acquired by "intimidation and extralegal appropriation of range land, actions that infuriated homesteaders and owners of smaller ranches," according to Jones. He used spot homesteading of sections containing water to limit the need for buying the whole expanse. So he used the public grassland, fencing some of it off for his 20 to 40 thousand cattle. Then the Kincaid Act of 1904 sent a wave of settlers into his domain.

The "Sandhills War" began with shootings and murder. One corpse lost its head which was replaced by another head. The jury decided this was not the murdered man and acquitted the accused. Richards and co-owners paid fines and went to jail for fencing-in public land. He died age 49 of an intestinal blockage before finishing his sentence. However, parts of his story are the fiction of several Hollywood westerns.

His son, Bartlett, Jr., wrote a well-documented biography and defense of his father which was published by the University of Nebraska after the son's death: *Bartlett Richards, Nebraska Sandhills Cattleman*. The major conflict centered on the inability of those in the east including eastern Nebraska to comprehend the ecologic uniqueness of the Sandhills. The ranchers attempt to get Congress to pass laws which would protect the public grasslands by leasing them failed. Instead, Congress wanted homesteaders to divide the vast acreage into homesteads and chop into the fragile hills with their plows. Within 20 years of Richard's death, leasing of Federal land was approved. One hundred years later, the battle between preserving fragile land and raising cattle is still going on: "A Strategy to Restore Western Grasslands Meets With Local Resistance" (New York Times, 12-1-2005, p A20.)

One of Richard's antagonists was "Old Jules" Sandoz, described as "a hardheaded Swiss" and father of the chronicler of the hills, Mari Sandoz. She suffered her father's prohibition against her writing. Her estrangement from the family, hard financial times, and numerous rejection letters from publishers prefaced her fame.

Jules Sandoz homesteaded in 1884; married and divorced three times; and constantly battled the ranchers, target shooting within sight of Spade Ranch to provoke Richards. Mari, the eldest of six children, listened to his stories as she traveled with him or sat around the stove at night. Her uncle had been shot in the back by a cowboy. That also became part of her story telling.

On his death bed, Jules asked Mari if she would write his life. She did: *Old Jules*. Published, it won the Atlantic Prize for nonfiction in 1935. *Crazy Horse, Cheyenne Autumn, Loving the Plains*, among many other books, followed as well as many short pieces preserved by the University of Nebraska.

She died in 1966. Much of her life is preserved in Gordon and at her home south of town on state highway 27 near the Old Spade ranch.

The Sandhills have suffered several invasions over the last two centuries. Will the hills absorb the new invasion of big money? Not only is the Niobrara Scenic River washed over by the wave of summer use ($15 million a year into Cherry County), but also absentee landowners are buying up large tracts of land. Media mogul Ted Turner has at least 170,000 acres in Sheridan County on which to run his buffalo. Canadian money is rumored to be finding its way into the hills. Land is becoming too expensive for the small rancher and it's driving up taxes. One wonders what Old Jules would have to say and perhaps do about present conditions.

CHAPTER FOUR:
WYOMING (1890)

And scarce had Wyoming of war or crime
Heard, but in transatlantic story rung,
For here the exile met from every clime,
And spoke in friendship every distant tongue:
Men from the blood of warring Europe sprung
Were but divided by the running brook;
And happy where no Rhenish trumpet sung,
On plains no sieging mine's volcano shook,
The blue-eyed German changed his sword to pruning-hook.
From Gertrude of Wyoming by Thomas Campbell, 1809

Wyoming is a geologist's paradise. The whole birth and maturation of the earth can be viewed in the different striations of rock from Archean to the present. The geologic progression reminds one of Disney's *Fantasia* and the thump, thump, thumping of Stravinsky's Rite of Spring. Mountains lift up and are covered by the vomit from volcanoes located in the future states of Idaho, Oregon, and Nevada. Oceans appear and disappear with the marine algae and plant life that will become the oil, coal, and gas extracted today. Pump Jacks, those contraptions bowing to the earth every few seconds, sip riches laid down eons ago. Wind. Unrelenting wind scourers the rock sending any soil to the east. Wyoming is the second highest state and the least populated. It is difficult to believe that it was once at sea level.

Entering Wyoming from the east, the traveler has no inkling of the geologic upheavals to be encountered. The passage to Douglas, Casper and Shoshoni is through high plains. Gen. Henry Dodge (the same as in the Black Hawk War) mapped the route of the Union Pacific Railroad over this formation known as "the gangplank" through the Laramie Range. He followed a buffalo trail.

Then there is the climb to Thermopolis through a finger of the Owl Creek Mountains and into the Bighorn Basin framed by the Bighorn Range on the east and the Tetons of the Rockies on the west. After Cody, the traveler enters the bubbling landscape of Yellowstone. This area is passing over a global hot spot creating the phantasmagoria of the first National Park.

The first sign in Wyoming tells the traveler that the road is 20 to Yellowstone National Park. Farther on the Texas Trail Marker indicates the movement of cattle from Texas to Wyoming and Montana "to replace the vanishing Buffalo and bring civilization to the western plains (1876-1897)." The traveler may have images of Larry McMurtry's novel *Lonesome Dove* upon reading this.

The Stage Coach Museum in Lusk is worth a stop featuring a stage used on the famed Cheyenne-Black Hills Stage Line to the gold fields. A collection of buggies, relics and an old store front are also displayed.

After Lusk, 20 passes over sediments only 20-25 million years old consisting of sandstone and claystone mixed with ash from distant volcanoes, before it joins interstate

25 south of Douglas. Here U.S. 20 meets the Oregon Trail at Orin on I-25. As the interstate approaches Douglas, a large silhouette of a jackalope greets the traveler from a hill. Yes, the jackalope, a cross between an antelope and a jack rabbit, is a figure of Western myth. Actually, the "horns" on the jack rabbits are caused by a wart virus.

Douglas prospered with the arrival of the Fremont, Elkhorn and Missouri Railroad which we have met before in Nebraska. Outside of Douglas, Fort Fetterman State Historic Site is described as "the last fort of its kind built in the Rockies." The Fort Fetterman marker describes the building named after who was killed in a battle with Sioux during Red Cloud's War, 1866. Major William Dye and several companies of the 4th Infantry began construction in July of 1867 using building parts and materials from the abandoned Fort Caspar (see below). Construction continued under various commanders into the 1870s. Then, well established, the post served a conspicuous part in the upcoming 1876 Indian campaigns.

A post commander in 1873 complained, "This is being one of the most remote and one of the most uninhabitable posts in the department." It is also where Gen. Custer left for his final battle in 1876.

"Although a hardship post, Fetterman was the only community within 50 to 100 miles. Its hospital, theater, sutler's store and garrison served the area ranchers, farmers, travelers, and Indians alike. Numerous colorful personalities of the time frequented the post including Jim Bridger, Wild Bill Hickok, Calamity Jane, Buffalo Bill Cody, Rain-In-The-Face and Alfred Packer." Packer, a survivor among a group of starving trappers, was found guilty of cannibalism in Colorado, escaped to Wyoming where he served time for the deed. He was formally pardoned of his crimes in 1981. Not far from the town of Fetterman was the infamous Hog Ranch named for the women (hogs) who worked at the gambling/dance "resort."

FORT FETTERMAN

In 1876, the Sioux War began in earnest and Fort Fetterman was the staging area for General George Crook's three campaigns. The first, in March, ended with the Reynold's fight on the Powder River. The second led to the Rosebud Fight on June 17, 1876, in southern Montana, Custer's Last Stand. The Indian victory was followed by the starvation march to South Dakota. The third concluded with Ronald Mackenzie's fight on the Red Fork of the Powder River in November (also known as the Dull Knife Battle) resulting in the final defeat of the Northern Cheyennes. (See the North brothers in chapter seven.)

Commenting on this campaign Gen. Crook said, "Yes, they are hard. But the hardest thing is to go out and fight against those who you know are in the right." (*Rising from the Plains*, page 20)

COAL TRAINS

Douglas is a good place to take a breather and talk about coal and coal trains. Along most of our trip we have traveled along side railroad tracks. Between Epworth and Dyersville Iowa we saw a loaded Burlington Northern Santa Fé coal train coming east; it appeared several miles long. It was coming from Powder River Basin coal fields. Most of these trains head farther south through North Platte Nebraska. But Wyoming coal from the Thunder Basin coal fields, part of the Powder River Basin, can end up from Michigan to Texas and any state in between.

To capture the flavor of this vast deposit of carbon one must picture a different landscape one hundred million years ago during the Cretaceous period. A huge swamp of green plant life falling on itself to pile layer upon layer of vegetation began the creation of coal. Climate changed and earth was piled on this mountain of matter compressing it, heating it and turning it into fuel for the furnaces of America.

Farther up state road 59 past Fort Fetterman is Bill, resident population one, the gateway to the largest coal field in the world. At the present rate of use, it can supply coal for the next 200 years. Its exploitation is the result of the Clean Air Act of 1970 which required that coal fired electric plants reduce the amount of sulfur released into the atmosphere. Companies deemed it cheaper to use the less sulfur containing coal, that also produced less energy, than to install scrubbers. So a new 100-mile Orin Line was built to the Wyoming coal fields where Thunder Basin National Grasslands is located. A new Grand Canyon is being dug with drag lines the size of three story houses and haul trucks the size of locomotives worthy of featuring on the Discovery Channel.

Outside of Bill, the coal cars are each loaded with 15 tons as they move under a chute. The train may consist of 130 cars or more and stretch more than one and one half miles. About 23,000 of these train loads leave Bill every year passing through Douglas. Some 1300 of these head for Macon, Georgia, and "the largest coal fired plant in the Western Hemisphere." From North Platte, the train passes through Maryville, Kansas, the Ozarks, Memphis, Chattanooga, and the Inman Yard in Atlanta before it births its load at Plant Scherer, Georgia. The trip will take five days to deliver the amount of coal that will be burned in less than eight hours for the air conditioning and neon of Greater Atlanta.

CASPER, NATRONA COUNTY

5,340 mi^2, 12 persons/mi^2

One highlight of our trek comes naturally at the American Trails Interpretive Center in Casper. It has easy access off and on I-25 and opens at 8am. The Center is hands-on, interactive with enough to keep a family busy for over an hour. The media show itself lasts a short 17 minutes describing the travels of the Native Americans in the area and the first incursions by the fur trappers and the missionaries. Then the travails of the Oregon Trail, the Mormon Trail and the California Trail are spoken in the words of the travelers. Visitors can climb in a covered wagon and experience a virtual attempt to cross the North Platte near the present Casper. The stagecoach, the pony express and the coming of the railroad complete the exposition.

Philip L. Fradkin described the ardors of stagecoach travel from Missouri to California: The travel lasted "some sixteen to twenty days or very likely more (including travel at night), mix in frequent accidents, incessant jolting, a thick coating of fine dust, lack of air-conditioning or heat, very little sleep, the lurking presence of trigger-happy robbers and vengeful Indians, and a ticket price up to eighteen times greater than what it now costs to fly from Missouri to California." (*Stagecoach, Wells Fargo and the American West*) This mode of transportation lasted about 11 years until the railroads replaced it.

From a history of Casper, "At Casper, Oregon Trail travelers had to cross the North Platte River in order to follow the Sweetwater River for the next portion of their trek. The Platte crossing was so dangerous during spring floods that the Mormons built a ferry, which was soon followed by a toll bridge. A small fort called Platte Bridge Station housed soldiers who protected the area."

Soldiers under the command of Lieutenant Caspar Collins ran into a large number of Lakota warriors under Red Cloud looking for revenge after the Sand Creek Massacre of Black Kettle's village, then under military protection. During the spring of 1865 (about the time Gen. Lee surrendered at Appomattox), the Southern, Arapaho and Powder River Sioux began raiding. After a few minor raids, they decided to destroy the Platte River Bridge. Sent from the bridge to rescue a military supply train, the lieutenant became a dead hero within sight of the bridge. The Fort was renamed for him. It became Caspar because Fort Collins, Colorado, was named for his father.

The fort, rebuilt by the Civilian Conservation Corps, contains replicas of army life similar to Fort Dodge. However, the museum on site expands on the history of Casper. The replica of a sheepherder's wagon is an obvious precursor to the modern travel home.

The city of Casper was established in 1888, eleven years after Fort Caspar was abandoned. Some obscure person misspelled Caspar as Casper, but the town is named for the fort. Casper's early years were violent ones. Its first mayor killed his business partner in a shootout on Main Street. Casper's earliest sales clerks, who slept in their stores in order to protect the goods, stacked flour sacks around their beds to help stop stray bullets. (Sounds familiar to the situation in Crawford, Nebraska.) Soon the city council adopted an ordinance making it "unlawful for any woman to frequent or remain in the barroom of any saloon in the town of Casper between the hours of 7 A.M. and 10 P.M." The prostitutes had control of the night. Apparently, the law was unenforceable because it was dropped in 1898.

From a Chamber of Commerce History: "The Casper vicinity has long been noted for its oil. In 1851 Jim Bridger, Kit Carson, and others found an oil spring on Poison Spider Creek west of Casper. Mixed with flour, the oil was marketable even at that early date as an axle grease for emigrant's wagons. By 1894 Casper had a small refinery and when Wyoming's first gusher was drilled in the Salt Creek Field in 1908, Casper's destiny was set as a boom and bust oil town. The first big boom lasted through the 1920's, and the optimism and affluence of that era can still be seen in the large gracious homes that remain on the 900 to 1200 blocks of South Center, Wolcott, Durbin, and Beech Streets."

Just 40 miles north of Casper is the Teapot Dome formation made infamous by the political scandal involving President Warren Harding's Secretary of the Interior, Albert Fall, and his friends Harry Sinclair and Edward Doheney. Fall turned over the oil under the dome to Sinclair for $304,000 cash in spite of its designation as naval oil reserve lands. Doheny got oil reserves in California for $105,000 cash. Fall went to jail for lying to the Senate; Sinclair cleared $25 million on the dome and Doheny cleared $100 million on the California oil field. This was one of the many scandals that tarnished the administration.

There is much more to see around Casper: museums, and side trips along the Oregon-California-Mormon-Pony Express Trail to Independence Rock and the Mormon Hand Car Visitors Center. Some of the names hammered into Independence Rock are replicated at the entrance to the National Historic Trails Interpretive Center. But we will stick to our plans and head out on 20 to Shawnee.

The "Old Yellowstone Highway," designated in the late 1920s, was originally from Denver to the park passing through Casper, Thermopolis, Worland, then Cody to the East Entrance. Later it was called "Park to Park" as it was to link up with Mesa Verde. The highway from the West Entrance to Oregon was not designated until 1942. We learned earlier that Lena, Illinois, won the highway by calling it the "Atlantic Yellowstone and Pacific Trail." This is not to be confused with the Yellowstone Trail which is essentially I-90 today and never directly reaches Yellowstone Park.

HELL'S HALF ACRE

Leaving Casper, 20 passes through cattle, antelope and deer country, and sand hills similar to those in Nebraska. Situated like statues along the highway, the wild animals seem to be spectators watching the traffic go by. One stop at Hell's Half Acre revealed a miniature Grand Canyon where the Native Americans chased buffalo to fall to their deaths.

The road sign identifies it as "A spectacular example of wind and water erosion. Hell's Half Acre is a geologic oddity – a craggy horseshoe-shaped gorge that drops away from an otherwise flat plain. The 150+ ft. deep gorge -- actually 320-acres total as it spreads south -- is filled, in one section, with jagged rock spires, naturally sculpted into nightmarish chaos by an ancient offshoot of the Powder River. Alien bug planet scenes for the movie *Starship Troopers* (1997) were filmed here. The crew spent weeks one summer hauling props down into the hole and shooting among the gnarled rock protrusions."

A return visit a year later revealed that the area was closed. The intrepid explorer can easily park at the entrance and walk to the edge of the gorge.

Passing through a small cluster of buildings called Moneta (population 5) recalls a battle between the Arapahos and a combined force of Shoshone warriors and army nearby. The engagement was a draw. The last Indian battle occurred in 1903 east of Bull on Lance Creek with fatalities among the posse and the Lakota.

SHOSHONI, CONVERSE COUNTY

2.83 persons per square mile

Shoshoni (note the difference in spelling from the tribal name) appears to be a dying town. We stopped at the drug store for lunch. It is stocked with the usual tourist gimcracks. The only other visitor said that they had been stopping there to eat for many years. This time they brought their grandson. Shoshoni hosts the Wyoming State Championship Old-time Fiddle Contest and the Flywheelers Antique Engine and Tractor Show.

In the summer of 1904, the Pioneer Townsite Company laid out the plat for Shoshoni. Shoshoni is an Indian word, which translates into "little snow." The first business to be erected in the town was the Elkhorn Hotel, built in September 1905. In less than a year, the town had become a tent city and had grown in population to approximately 2,000.

Lack of building material in the very early days was a problem, because the railroad -- Chicago and Northwestern - was 100 miles away. Nevertheless, the town gradually grew in size. Unfortunately, Shoshoni was devastated by fires in 1907 and 1908. During the reconstruction, brick buildings took the place of flammable wood structures.

In its boom days Shoshoni boasted 23 saloons, two banks, two large mercantile establishments, several livery and feed stables, a lumber yard, drug store, two physicians, several lawyers, a newspaper and more lodging houses and restaurants than any town of equal size in the state of Wyoming according to one history.

In the town center, the traveler can make the choice of continuing on 20 to Cody and Yellowstone Park or 26 to Jackson and Idaho Falls where 20 can be joined again.

If one draws a line on a Wyoming map from Casper to Lost Cabin, to Thermopolis, along the Big Horn River to Mendelson, then Burlington, and finally Fannie on the border with Montana, it will trace the Bridger Trail. Mountain man Jim Bridger considered this route through the Big Horn Basin much safer than the route John Bozeman selected through the Powder River Basin. Bridger was right. (See chapter seven)

THERMOPOLIS, HOT SPRINGS COUNTY

The county population is 4,854, 2 per square mile, 90% white, 1.5 % Native American

The highway begins its climb up the Wind River Canon. The river has cut through several layers of geologic history. Signs along the road mark the geologic age when the rock was laid down. The drive is spectacular cutting Precambrian granite, gneiss and schist born about two billion years ago. Then, Cambrian shale, next Triassic bright red siltstone to layers of limestone, dolomite, followed by Jurassic layers, then Cretaceous layers of sandstone and shale and finally Tertiary volcanic rock merging to shale and sandstone. It is as if a slice of a massive layer cake had been removed to expose the building process of the earth.

Farther on 20, Thermopolis is a bustling tourist town with many amenities including the Wyoming Dinosaur Center & Dig Sites, Dancing Bear Folk Center, Hot Springs County Historical Museum, Hot Springs County Museum, Old West Wax Museum, and the Hot Springs State Park which is open to the public for a dip in the waters at several venues. Here hot water dissolves calcium carbonate and it precipitates out as it cools "making the hot springs a natural cement factory."

Thermopolis was originally part of the Wind River Indian Reservation. The Shoshone and Arapaho Tribes sold this land to the United States, so the healing waters of the Big Horn Hot Springs would be available to all people. Thus, the State Park containing the springs has no fee.

The Wyoming Dinosaur Center and Dig Sites provide a unique opportunity to discover this prehistoric world before Ashfall. The center is a 16,000 square foot complex. It includes a world-class museum, working dig sites and a complete modern preparation laboratory. An interpretive dig site tour allow visitors to walk the same ground as ancient dinosaurs and watch as scientists remove fossils from burial sites.

The Hot Springs County Museum and Cultural Center takes you on a journey to the earliest settlers in the county. Hot Springs County saw the first cabin, the first industry – cattle raising – the first coal mining, early agriculture, and some of the earliest petroleum production in the Basin. Period rooms at the Museum include the cherry wood bar from the Hole-In-The-Wall Saloon, a favorite hangout for Butch Cassidy and the Sundance Kid.

When early explorers went through the Big Horn Basin, they saw that all the water drained into what they would call the Big Horn River. Explorers from the South came through the Wind River Mountains and named the river found there the Wind River. Each group did not know that the other group had named the same river. The river changes names at the Wedding of the Waters just a few miles south of Thermopolis. Here the river leaves the Wind River behind and becomes the Big Horn River. The river flows lazily through Thermopolis with many public floating, fishing and bird hunting accesses. Tourism, oil and gas, farming, ranching, recreation and health care support the economy of Thermopolis.

Here the traveler has a choice of taking the 120 shortcut to Cody or continuing on 20. We chose 20. The road follows the Big Horn River to Worland.

WORLAND, WASHAKIE COUNTY

Washakie County is named for a Shoshone Chief who continued to be friendly with the whites during the Indian Wars (see chapter seven). The county population is 7,883, 90% white, 11.5 % Hispanic, 3.7 persons per acre.

In the center of town, a statue of a woman wearing a pioneer bonnet and throwing seed from a sack grabs attention. At the site is a carved rock containing a dedication to the settling of Worland. Charles H. "Dad" Worland dug a canal from the Big Horn River to use for irrigation "drawing pioneer men and women possessing an indomitable spiritual force dreaming that Big Horn River water would create a new way of life here in the desert. With muscles and guts, horses and handtools, they dug miles of irrigation canals. With precious water the parched land became an oasis. We cheer those who persevered and conquered the desert making Worland the jewel of the Big Horne Basin."

What isn't said is that the site of the famous Hole-in-the-Wall was established by Dad Worland as a stage stop and tavern selling whisky to Butch Cassidy and his gang. With the Hanover Canal and the arrival of the Burlington and Northern Railroad a town grew around the Worland homestead. Today the land grows sugar beets, beans, and barley for beer.

Outside of Worland is a huge factory processing bentonite, the volcanic ash dumped on the area. It absorbs 20 times its weight in water and is used by the drilling industry as well as in cat litter and Fuller's earth. Unfortunately, some volcanic ash contains a large amount of selenium. An invader to the area, the woody aster plant, extracts the selenium from the soil; cattle and sheep who eat the plants are poisoned as well as humans who eat the meat.

Between Worland and Greybull, the high desert is spotted with green irrigated patches and the ranches that oversee this transformation. During the 1880s and 90s, this cattle land was owned by English, German and Scottish absentee landlords. At Greybull, the traveler meets U.S. 14 to Cody and Yellowstone. The Bighorn Basin is "10,000 square miles of irrigated farms, oil wells, sagebrush, and badlands. Its development is limited by the 15 inches of average rainfall a year." Just a few miles northeast of Greybull is the Howe dinosaur quarry where several sauropod bodies were found in the 1930s including an Allosaurus skeleton, a precursor of Tyrannosaurus Rex.

Just west of town is the Greybull Museum of Flight which appears from the highway to be an airplane graveyard. Huge airplanes are scattered next to the runway. Greybull was first developed by Mormons who brought green to the arid desert with a massive canal project.

The highway, crossing the Bighorn Basin between Greybull and Cody, passes through what appears to be, and is, desolate desert. Sediments cover black shales of the upper Cretaceous Cody formation. A couple of signs along 20 identify it as part of the Bozeman Trail.

In 1863, John Bozeman and a partner split off the Oregon Trail near present-day Casper and headed north along the route of today's I-25. It turned west into the Big Horn Mountains and the gold fields that brought white incursion and Sioux and Cheyenne anger. The army established three forts in the area in 1866. Cap. William J. Fetterman fell into a trap outside of Fort Phil Kearny the same year and was killed along with 81 soldiers. It was the worst army disaster until Custer's 10 years later. As Red

Cloud's war developed, the trail became quite dangerous and was abandoned along with the forts after the Fort Laramie Treaty in 1868. The treaty lasted only three years until Custer's expedition discovered gold in the Black Hills.

The area around present-day Sheridan and the Powder River was the site of several other Indian battles. Apparently the army was learning to defend themselves and not to rush into battle. The battles of Wagon Box and Hayfield are typical. Having breach loading rifles and canons helped. Canons also helped at the Tongue River and the Little Powder River when 1000 of the same Indians involved in the Platte Bridge fight, where Lt. Caspar was killed, attacked a much smaller force.

CODY, PARK COUNTY

population 26,516, 96.5 % white

Colonel William F. "Buffalo Bill" Cody accompanied a Yale University professor in his studies of the West including the Big Horn Basin during the 1870s. Cody returned during the mid 1890's with friends to develop the land and build a community. These developers insisted on naming the town Cody. It also prospered, much like in Worland and Greybull, through the digging of irrigation canals. By 1902, the town was incorporated and Cody opened his hotel named for his youngest daughter, Irma. Cody got the Burlington Railroad to send up a spur and President Teddy Roosevelt to get the Bureau of Reclamation to build the Shoshone Dam and Reservoir: Eventually called The Buffalo Bill Dam.

The Buffalo Bill Historical Center on the main street through town is a necessary stop for those interested in the history of the West. Cody is a rodeo town with one going on every night and a stampede over the 4th of July. If you haven't had enough of frontier life, I recommend Old Trail Town on the way out of Cody if only to see the grave of "Liver Eating Johnson" better known from the film as "Jeremiah Johnson."

From Cody, 20 begins its climb along the Shoshone River, passing Buffalo Bill Dam and Reservoir to Yellowstone National Park where 20 temporally ends only to begin again at the west portal. The highway passes through tunnels carved out of the Precambrian rock of Rattlesnake Mountain. One might catch the odor of rotten eggs from the hot springs along the river preparing the traveler for Yellowstone. It gave the river its first name, Stinking Water River. Fifty million years before the present, volcanoes, similar to Mount St. Helens, erupted sending thick, muddy mixtures of rock and ash debris down. Erosion created strange castle-like structures out of the residue: hoodooos. These are volcanic leftovers that have weathered out from the surrounding softer rock. The structures along the canyon make the climb to the east portal interesting.

Although Yellowstone is a fantastic experience in nature's geologic varieties, we will hurry through so that we can travel U.S. 20 again. Nevertheless, the traveler following this trek is advised to take some time for the experience and to appreciate the astonishment of those who first entered this land of bubbling caldrons.

The traveler will be passing through the caldera of the Yellowstone volcano which covers the center of the park from the eastern to western boundaries including Yellowstone Lake. As can be seen, the caldera is still active as the continent moves over this thin hot spot. This "super volcano" resembling other volcanoes such as the one on the California-Nevada boarder, Long Valley, blew itself over all of the western U.S. about 640,000 years ago and could blow again any time.

****

The history of Wyoming mirrors its violent geologic history with the blood of Indian Wars, outlaws, cattle rustlers, and lynchings. The infamous hanging of Cattle Kate,

Ellen Watson, and her husband for cattle rustling by six prominent cattlemen is one example. The couple was homesteading on land the ranchers considered theirs. Then there was the Johnson County War (1890s) when a group of ranchers and their hired guns (the Regulators) went after the small ranchers. After killing two "resisters," the Regulators invaded Johnson County near the town of Buffalo. They were stopped by a large posse of local citizens and had to be rescued by the cavalry.

One exception to this violent view is the relationship with the Shoshone under the leadership of Chief Washakie. Although the tribe continued to lose their reservation land to white incursion and through sharing with their traditional enemies the Arapahos, they continued to support the whites. Shoshone scouts accompanied Gen. Crook's 1876 expedition that ended with the Battle of the Rosebud. The present Wind River Reservation covers 2.2 million acres with a little more than two thousand Shoshone and four thousand Arapahos living there.

Wyoming should also be remembered as the first territory to allow women's suffrage. It all started as a political joke. Democrats, thinking that the Republican territorial governor would not sign a law passed by a Democratic legislature, passed the women's suffrage law. The governor signed it, in 1869, and, when Wyoming became a state in 1890, suffrage prevailed.

CHAPTER FIVE:
IDAHO (1890)

"It was a desolate, dismal scenery. Up or down the valley as far as the eye could reach or across the mountains and into the dim distance the same unvarying mass of black rock. Not a shrub, bird nor insect seemed to live near it. Great must have been the relief of the volcano, powerful the emetic, that poured such a mass of black vomit." From one traveler on Goodale's Cutoff now Craters of the Moon NM

The topography of Idaho, similar to that of Wyoming, gives evidence of the slow, but inexorable, collisions of land: lifting up mountains, birthing volcanoes and redirecting the flow of water. It is also the land of fur trappers, mountain men, gold seekers, sheep herders, ranchers, Mormons, and miners. Few if any stayed here on the trek to Oregon. Only when gold was discovered did a few stay. When irrigation became available, farmers, mainly Mormons, and ranchers came and the rich volcanic soil yielded its famous potatoes among the diverse crops.

Outside of Yellowstone, 20 passes through West Yellowstone, Montana, and crosses the Continental Divide at Targhee Pass (named for a Bannock chief) near Henry's Fork of the Snake River. Here tourist laden stages from Virginia City, Montana, and Salt Lake City, Utah, began their entrance to the park. In 1908, an industrious bandit went down a row of 17 backed up stages collecting money and valuables. He was never caught.

The route west passes by Henrys Lake site of encampments for both Chief Joseph's Nez Pierce, on their attempted escape to Canada, and Gen. O.O. Howard's pursuing cavalry before they both entered what is now Yellowstone Park. In Yellowstone Park, the Nez Pierce shot one of the early tourists in the head. He survived. The Indians were escaping after the Battle of the Big Hole in Montana Territory where the calvary got beat but the natives lost many women and children. From Yellowstone, the Nez Pierce nearly crossed into Canada before surrendering to the cavalry.

At one time an estimated 90 thousand pounds of fish were taken from Henrys lake each winter and sent to the mining camps at Virginia City and Helena transported on the Utah & Northern Railroad.

Farther on, Island Park appears as an extended city through pine tree country dotted with convenience stores, gas stations and camp grounds for visitors to Yellowstone Park and Harriman State Park (day use only). The park is a gift from the railroad Harriman family. The uninformed traveler would not discern that the route crosses a two million-year-old caldera, the remains of a collapsed volcano. Farther on, a 25-mile side loop is recommended on state road 47 to see the Mesa Falls. Some say these falls are more spectacular than Niagara Falls.

Moving on to Ashton, the topography returns to high and dry desert sucking up irrigation water. Ashton is the source of the famous Russet Burbank seed potatoes. The next town, St. Anthony, is the site of the preparation by Wilson Price Hunt's voyage down the Snake River until the party reached the rapids of the Devil's Scuttle Hole almost to Twin Falls (1811). There the group decided to split up and head to Astoria by foot (see chapter seven). West of St. Anthony are some spectacular sand dunes.

The next small town down the highway is Rexburg. Originally a Mormon town, it now caters to summer travelers and claims an antique wooden carousel at Porter Park. The former Rexburg tabernacle (on the National Register of Historic Sites) contains a museum explaining the flood of 1976 when the new earthfill Teton Dam broke wiping out a good part of the town.

THE BATTLE OF PIERRE'S HOLE

According to several sources, including the April 1999 issue of *Wild West*, the Teton River was the scene of a much more famous story that appears to be missing in most histories of the area. The river, first called Pierre's Hole, was the site of the first rendezvous of trappers. State road 33 follows the river east to Teton Pass which was one of the main routes through the Rockies before the discovery of South Pass.

Apparently, John Colter in his wanderings over the Rockies discovered this green valley in 1808. Andrew Henry came through in 1810 before establishing his Fort near the present town of St. Anthony. This was lucrative beaver country. The Hunt and the MacKenzie corps came through on their treks. The river was named for trapper Pierre Trevantiagon who established a base of trapping operations between the present towns of Driggs and Victor. Trevantiagon and his company were rescued by Jedediah Smith in 1823 after they had been left destitute on the Portneuf River near the present city of Pocatello by Bannocks. However, the Blackfoot got him in 1828.

The battle began after the rendezvous of 1832 (8-18 July). More than 200 trappers with many lodges of Nez Perce and Flatheads congregated waiting for supplies from the east. Captain B.L.E. Bonneville appeared and wrote a description of the "motley populace" camped there.

Captain Bill Sublette arrived with alcohol and other necessary supplies on 180 mules along with 100 men including the tenderfoot Nathaniel Wyeth. Sublette's semi-military operation kept ahead of an expedition of American Fur Company suppliers. He who gets there first gets the pelts. Nevertheless, Sublette ran into Blackfoot and lost 10 horses. Thomas Fitzpatrick headed toward the east to hurry Sublette along and lost his horses, weapons, and nearly his scalp on the return trip to the rendezvous. It turned him white-headed.

As the rendezvous broke up, Bill Sublette's brother Milton's small band, including Wyeth, sighted a large group of Gros Ventre Indians carrying a British flag that they had taken from an ambushed Hudson Bay Company group. The trappers set up a fortification. The Indians sent a chief to parley. An Iroquois trapper sent to the parley killed the chief instead and the Indians set up their own fortification.

Bill Sublette arrived with more men and attacked the Indians with 60 volunteers. Heated exchanges of gunfire and arrows continued until most of the ammunition was exhausted. It turned into a standoff with the Indians abandoning the breastworks after dark. The possible site of this encounter is marked by a sign identifying it as being on the National Register of Historic Places.

Sublette, wounded in the arm, paused to heal his wound a bit, then headed east with nearly $85,000 worth of furs. He nearly lost them to some angry Gros Ventre but bought them off with 25 pounds of tobacco.

This was the last great rendevous at Pierre's Hole. The numbers of beaver were dwindling. When Mormons moved into the river valley during the late 1880s, the area became the Teton Valley. The river flows into the Snake River.

GOODALE'S CUTOFF

The Snake River defines the southern part of Idaho. The huge plain is bordered on the north by several ranges sticking their fingers into the edge of 20. The landscape is the result of titanic geologic disturbances. One thought is that the hot spot under Yellowstone was once under Idaho.

At Idaho Falls, U.S. 20 meets and quickly leaves I-15, known as the gold road following the route to the gold fields in the north. The city hosts the homes of many who work 50 miles west on 20 at the Idaho National Engineering Laboratory. The land along 20 quickly changes from potato farms to sagebrush and lava rock that soaks up any water. Betty Derig in her *Roadside History of Idaho* reports on Owl Cave west of Idaho Falls at the Wasden site. The archeologic site has yielded bones of bison, mammoths, camels and evidence of long human habitation.

The Oregon Trail met the Snake River at Fort Hall. There were several alternate routes one of which goes north from Fort Hall and connects with the present U.S. 20: Goodale's Cutoff. The Oregon Trail itself was the longest route across the west at 2,020 miles beginning in Independence, Missouri, and ending at Oregon City, Oregon. The eastern part of the trail should properly be called the Overland Trail since it consisted of many trails one of which went to Oregon. We'll stick with Oregon Trail since it is the one that 20 frequently encounters.

The cutoff was discovered by Donald McKensie's fur trade party in 1820. Most travelers stopped at Fort Hall near present Blackfoot. Goodale led 820 emigrants, 338 wagons and 1,400 head of livestock in 1862. The 230-mile spur headed north from Fort Hall toward Big Southern Butte, a conspicuous landmark on the Snake River Plain. From there it passed near the present-day town of Arco, wound through the northern part of Craters of the Moon National Monument, went southwest to Camas Prairie, and ended at Fort Boise. This journey typically took two to three weeks.

Goodale's Cutoff took its toll on the travelers and their wagons. The rugged lava restricted travel to one lane, so progress was slow. The path along the edge of the lava flows was circuitous. The emigrants typically passed through in late July, the hottest part of the summer. Wood dried out in the desert air and shrank, causing wheels and wagon boxes to come apart. Pioneers wrote of finding pieces of broken wagons littering the trail.

By 1862, the Northern Shoshone and Bannock tribes were beginning to resist the intrusion of settlers into their homeland. In August of that year, Bannock Indians ambushed a wagon train on the Oregon Trail at Massacre Rock, killing 10 people. The growing Indian hostility along the trail resulted in increased demand for a safe alternative. In 1863, seven out of every ten wagons en route from Fort Hall to Boise took Goodale's Cutoff instead of the main Oregon Trail. For nearly 50 years, westward-bound pioneers used Goodale's Cutoff. Later, miners moving ore to railroad depots and stagecoaches carrying passengers to the towns of southern Idaho took the route. Traveling 20 today is literally following those wooden wheels.

THE BEAR RIVER MASSACRE

Beginning in 1860, Mormon settler incursion into the Cache Valley on the border of Idaho and Utah, near the present village of Franklin, invaded Indian land. By 1863, the land and water had been appropriated by the settlers. Young men of the Shoshone tribe struck back and the Utah territorial officials called on the army based in Salt Lake City to do something.

Colonel Patrick "take no prisoners" Connor and about 200 California Volunteers attacked at daybreak and were initially repulsed. They surrounded the village and began shooting the women and children as the warriors ran out of ammunition. Few if any Indians escaped being shot, raped and their heads bashed in with axes. Ninety women and children were among those killed and left for "the wolves and the crows." The site is marked with a sign.

ARCO, BUTTE COUNTY

population 2,838, 94% white, 4% Latino

Our first stop on 20 is about 50 miles past Idaho Falls at the Historical marker: National Environmental Research Park Idaho National Engineering Lab (U.S. Department of Energy). It tells us that 1.5 million acres were established in 1975 devoted to atomic energy research. The marker touts the presence of a diversity of animals including morning doves, sage grouse and prong horn antelope. Interspersed among this diverse fauna are 50 nuclear reactors more than any where else in the word.

Arco sits on the finger of the Lost River Range. This river is aptly named because its flow frequently disappears only to reappear farther on. The town of Arco, Idaho, originally a stage stop at a road junction (1879), is hoping for the redevelopment of the National Reactor Testing Station, renamed the Idaho National Laboratory, to bring it back from a slow decline. The Department of Energy has published plans to make plutonium here again. The ranchers and tradesmen having morning coffee at the Pickle Place, "Home of the Atomic Berger," are hoping for employment at the site just a few miles south. The ranchers are the descendants of those participating in the 1909 Enlarged Homestead act opening the land west for land drawings.

The town appears stagnant or deteriorating. State Historical Site #152 in the town park proclaims, "An important page in atomic history was written here on July 17, 1955 when the lights of Arco were successfully powered from atomic energy." From the number of motels in the town, the highway appears heavily traveled. There is a beautiful stone church along the highway. Each high school graduating class has written its year on the butte facing town.

Drought has forced many of the ranchers along U.S. 20 west of Arco to sell their ranches or sell off their cattle. Beside the INL, the town relies on a few tourists traveling to The Craters of the Moon National Monument. While the local people need the employment, the people farther east are fearful of the "fallout." On one level, it would appear that the wealthy of Jackson Hole are pitted against the less affluent residents of Arco and vicinity.

Past Arco, the Lost River Valley becomes cattle country dotted with a few feedlots along the highway. As we approach Craters of the Moon, the land becomes more desolate.

CRATERS OF THE MOON NATIONAL MONUMENT

Established by Presidential proclamation in 1924, Craters of the Moon National Monument has been enlarged by additional proclamations. The expanded Monument and Preserve are co-managed by the National Park Service and the Bureau of Land Management. A sea of lava-flows with scattered islands of cinder cones and sagebrush identifies this "weird and scenic landscape." The park contains three major lava fields covering almost half a million acres. This rough terrain of lava was used by the Apollo astronauts to become familiar with the geology that they might encounter on the moon. It can remind one of a Hawaiian landscape with its lava tubes.

The Visitor's Center is worth a stop along the highway. There is a charge for entrance and camping. The center provides interpretive programs and geologic explanations. A loop road leads into the landscape and various sites including a cave. About a quarter of a million visitors a year pass through, summer and winter. There are trails for hiking and bicycling. The last volcanic eruption occurred about 2,000 years ago but you won't find a volcano. Instead the lava pushes up through cracks in the crust. We will see this up-welling again in south central and eastern Oregon.

A historical marker identifying Goodale's cutoff and describing the extreme difficulties in passing over the jagged rock rests along side the road. Upon leaving the park the ruts of the wagons that traveled the cutoff can be seen heading west toward Carey.

At Carey, a somewhat larger small town, US 26, which we picked up south of Arco, leaves 20 to head south. We continue on to Picabo noted for its trout fishing and Nature Conservancy land at Silver Creek. We cross state route 75 from Twin Falls to Ketchum and Sun Valley, and enter Magic City with its reservoir. The area depends on a heavy snow fall for irrigation of farms near Shoshone, south of 20. Farther on a roadside marker explains The Bannock War. Indians protesting the encroachment of settlers on Comas Prairie, which had been guaranteed to them, began a rampage through the territory. Chief Buffalo Horn lead his band to war in 1878.

We passed through the little towns of Corra and Fairfield. Each had a couple of restaurants and just a few houses. Fairfield in Camas County sits at the end of the Sawtooth range. The camas plain was once covered with blue camas flowers now supplanted by grazing and alfalfa fields. The bulbs of these flowers were edible and their destruction by white incursion initiated the Bannock War.

THE BANNOCK WAR

This war in 1878 is similar to the others in that it was caused by the maltreatment of the Indians. According to the Fort Bridger Treaty Council of 1868, the Bannocks were restricted to the Fort Hall Reservation. They suffered famine due to white poachers killing cattle and insufficient rations. General George Crook assessed that "[I]t was not surprise . . . that some of the Indian [sic] soon afterward broke out into hostilities, and the great wonder is that so many remained on the reservation. With the Bannocks and Shoshone, our Indian policy has resolved itself into a question of war path or starvation, and being merely human, many of them will always choose the former alternative when death shall at least be glorious."

Hostilities began when two white men were wounded by a Bannock in August 1877 and a murder of a white man in November. The next spring the Bannocks, Paiutes and Shoshone gathered to dig camas roots at Camas Prairie. When they arrived, they found all the roots eaten by hogs belonging to whites. The son of one of the chiefs, Buffalo Horn, wounded two white men who were driving 2,500 cattle across the prairie. Some of the Indians rushed back to their reservation. Two hundred others, led by Buffalo Horn, decided to drive out the white man.

As they ranged through southern Idaho killing whites, they arrived at Silver City. During the shootout Buffalo Horn was killed. Leaderless, they headed for Oregon adding Paiutes, Oytes and Egan warriors thus increasing the band to 450. Negotiations with a Paiute chief's daughter failed. The band was surprised on June 23 by three troops of cavalry. Some escaped to the hills. General Oliver Howard pursued fighting several battles until the remaining Indians were subdued and 131 sent back to the reservation on September 12. This war ranged from Idaho to Oregon to Wyoming and is considered by some as the last Indian war in that area.

But was it? In 1870, five Chinese prospectors were killed and later two white prospectors north of Boise near the present city of Grangeville on the Salmon River. The killers may have been remnants of the Bannocks known as Sheepeaters or Weisers. One column of soldiers was ambushed by a smaller force under the leadership of War Jack. Eventually, the small party of 30 Indians was chased until forced to surrender. This brief confrontation was known as the Sheepeater War.

This is cattle country with circle irrigation. Hill City contains just four or five homes. The next historical marker identifies a gold mining area: Rocky Bar, Happy Camp and other South Boise mining towns 30 minutes northwest. The towns were established in 1863. Nearby, we cross Sawtooth Pass, at more than 5000 feet and pass through the Pleasant Valley and Running Bear Resort. To the right is the Anderson Dam and recreation area.

Driving through high chaparral, we descend past a marker for the junction of a stage coach stop at Rattle Snake Road. This is where the cutoff rejoined the Oregon Trail and the original site of Mountain Home. When the railroad came through a few miles west of the town, Mountain Home moved but retained its name. Here the traveler is taken into Boise on interstate 84.

BOISE, ADA COUNTY

1,055 mi^2, population 285/mi^2 Bosie sits at the base of the Salmon River Range

When John Reid built his trading post at the mouth of the Boise River in 1813, Bannock Indians killed him and destroyed the fort.

In 1834, the Hudson's Bay Company backed Thomas McKay in building Fort Boise at the junction of the Snake and Boise Rivers near the present town of Parma about 40 miles northeast of the present city of Boise. Theodore Talbot, a traveler on the Oregon Trail wrote in1843, "We came to the Fort which is situated on Snake River, immediately below the mouth of the Boise River. This Fort which is one of the smallest we have visited, is neatly constructed of Adobes and belongs to the Hud. [sic] Bay Company. Capt. Payette the gentleman in charge is a Frenchman and exceedingly polite, courteous and hospitable. He is a veteran in the service of the Hud. Bay Company. Has travelled much and undergone many hardships, in consideration of which his valuable services, he has been placed in charge of this post."

Joel Palmer, another traveler wrote on September 2, 1845, "We reached Fort Boise. This is a trading post of the Hudson's Bay Company, established upon the northern side of Snake or Lewis River, and about one mile below the mouth of the Boise river. This fort was erected for the purpose of recruiting, or as an intermediate post, more than as a trading point. It is built of the same materials, and modeled after Fort Hall, but is of a smaller compass. Portions of the bottoms around it afford grazing; but in a general view, the surrounding country is barren . . . At this fort they have a quantity of flour in store, brought from Oregon City, for which they demanded twenty dollars per cut, in cash . . . At this place the road crosses the river, the ford is about four hundred yards below the fort, and strikes across to the head of an island, then bears to the left to the southern bank; the water is quite deep, but not rapid . . . "

The fort was made of adobe and a Boise River flood in 1853 destroyed it. The chronology of the happenings around the fort suggests that some attempt was made to rebuild it. If the traveler takes 20/26 through Boise, the site of the Middleton massacre is marked by a park and signs at the corner of Middleton and Lincoln Roads. The Alexander Ward party was camped at noon in 1854 when a band of Indians approached and a horse was grabbed; shots were fired; and the wagon train was set upon. The people, including women and children, were killed, mutilated and burned. This attack caused the closing of the Hudson Bay forts at Boise and Hall.

In 1863, Maj. Pinckney Lugenbeel established another Fort Boise on the Boise River at the present site of the city. The little town was incorporated in 1864 and boasted the second newspaper in the state, the *Idaho Statesman*.

Noting the thirsty miners and cowboys, John Lemp, a German immigrant, opened a brewery the same year. He was known as the "Beer King of Idaho" and lived until 1912. When the gold rush ended, the town's population declined briefly then grew with the need for a federal mint and the Idaho Penitentiary. The penitentiary was closed in 1973 and is now the home of the Idaho Botanical Gardens. There is also the Basque Museum recognizing their emigration into the area.

On up I-84, where Caldwell is now, a summer Indian trading place was located. Nez Perce brought their horses, Paiute, arrowheads, Umatilla and Cayuse brought ornamental seashells from the Pacific Coast, Shoshone, buffalo hides. Cheyennes and Arapaho also made their appearance.

The last leg of our journey to the coast begins when we cross I-84 having passed a historic site sign telling us of the emigrant crossing of the Boise River. This sign claims that "the route is still visible" at Cannon Hill. In 1853 Maria Bradshaw wrote that she crossed the ford "15 rods wide and three feet deep with a gravel bottom and salmon." For some time we will follow the Oregon Trail on 20 signed as an auto tour.

PARMA, CANYON COUNTY

The county also serves as a bedroom community for Boise with a population of 223/mi^2, 95% white

Entering Parma, the replica of Fort Boise stands out. There is overnight camping. The fort itself is open on weekends in the summer, 1:00 to 3:00 p.m., sponsored by the Old Fort Boise Historical Society. According to one sign, the fort was established in 1834 as a Hudson Bay post on the Snake River. As described earlier, a flood in 1853 washed away the adobe building and Indian trouble forced abandonment two years later although farming had been successful around the fort.

Another sign tells the story of Marie Dorion, an Iowa Indian, and her two children who were the only survivors of a Bannock Indian raid of a fur trade expedition six miles farther west in 1814. This was the Reid trading post. She set out on a 200-mile journey through the snow and was finally rescued by Wala Wala Indians. A statue of her and her two children sits near the entrance to the fort.

A statue of a rather fierce Indian stands nearby. It is a real Big Foot, a scourge of the country from 1856 to 1868 when he was killed with 16 bullets. Unfortunately, his death was not reported for 10 years so he existed as a ghost terrorizing the locals during that interval.

CHAPTER SIX:
OREGON (1859)

"[Indian war] is the natural result of immigration and settlement . . . The history of our Indian wars will show that the primary cause is the progress of civilization, to which the inferior races, from their habits and instincts, are naturally opposed." J. Ross Browne, "Indian War in Oregon and Washington Territories," U.S. House Doc. 38, 35 Cong., 1858

U.S. 20 crosses the Snake River at Nyssa, Oregon, and heads for Ontario combined with 26 again. Before Ontario, 20 goes west and 26 heads north. This country relies on both spray and canal irrigation. In Idaho, I saw some cattle standing under the spray keeping cool, or taking a shower, and viewed the same activity along the road to Vale. Malheur Butte is on the left, a modest indicator of the basalt volcanoes to come. From here to Vale the basalt flows are covered with deep sediment conducive to the agriculture.

Oregon was quite tropical during the Miocene age with an inland sea where 20 travels through now.

Passing through Vale it is noteworthy that the Oregon Trail crossed the Malheur River here before heading north. US 20 follows the river all the way up the mountain rise to Juntura. The rise and fall of the route passes through green, irrigated valleys and sage brush dotted hills. Along some road-cuts the variety of geologic formation, a blending of igneous and sedimentary rock, is visible. The county is 94 percent rangeland. The Bureau of Land Management is landlord of 72% of the county. Irrigated fields in the county's northeast corner, known as Western Treasure Valley, are the center of intensive and diversified farming. Malheur County's economy also depends on tourism.

As the elevation increases one can appreciate the transitions of vegetation into pine tree country. Soon we reach Drink Water Pass then Stinkingwater Pass and descend into the Harney Basin passing Stink Water Creek. Another sign describing the Bannock Wars, similar to the one on Goodale's Cutoff, appears. The pursuit and fighting occurred north and south of 20. Gen. George Crook clashed with the Snake Indians more than 50 times chasing them around southeast Oregon and southwest Idaho for two years before subduing them in 1868.

The Indians in this area did not have horses and existed on "roots, nuts, fish and small game." White settlements were fair game and Fort Boise was too far away to be much help. The army's ability to chase the perpetrators, according to a Boise Editor, "is like hunting ducks with a brass band." Crook decided to stay "in the field" until the Indians either were dead or subdued.

North of 20 around Antelope is "Zane Grey Country," where the author based some of his westerns. It is also the location of the short lived Bhagwan Shree Rajneesh cult's land before it reverted to desert.

BURNS, HARNEY COUNTY

This county averages 1 person per mi^2

Burns, is the only town on this stretch of 20 with more than three or four buildings. "Harney County was carved out of the southern two-thirds of Grant County on February 25, 1889. A fierce political battle, with armed night riders who spirited county records from Harney to Burns, ended with Burns as the county seat in 1890." The Malheur River Indian Reservation was created by executive order on March 14, 1871, and the Northern Paiute Indians within the Oregon state boundaries were settled there.

As 20 crosses a rise outside of Burns, the snow capped volcanoes, the Three Sisters, stick their majestic heads out of the Cascade Range in the distance. Glass Butte (6385 feet), a mountain of obsidian (beautiful volcanic rock), sits on the left of the highway. It is still a long way to Bend

BEND, Deschutes County

2005 population 140,161. an increase of 7.8% in five years

Bend is a surprise for the traveler: a large town at the bend of the Deschutes River. During the 1990s, Deschutes County experienced the most rapid growth of any county in Oregon largely due to the availability of year-round recreational activities. Beyond tourism, principal industries in the county are lumber, ranching and agriculture--chiefly potatoes. The Forest Service owns 51% of the lands within the county boundaries.

Until the winter of 1824, the Bend area was known only to Native Americans who hunted and fished there. In that year, members of a fur trapping party led by Peter Skene Ogden visited the area. John C. Fremont, Dr. John Strong Newberry and other Army survey parties came next. Then pioneers heading farther west went through the area and forded the Deschutes River at what was then called Farewell Bend.

Actual settlement did not occur until the early 1900s. A small community developed around the bend in the river and in 1904 a city was incorporated by a general vote of the community's 300 residents. On January 4, 1905, the city held its first official meeting as an incorporated municipality, appointing A. H. Goodwillie as the first mayor.

A short side trip south from Bend on U.S. 97 affords opportunity to understand the ecology and geology of the Cascades at the High Desert Museum. The Newberry National Volcanic Monument lies farther south on 97. Every turn entices the traveler to take in side trips such as the Cascades Lakes Highway National Forest Scenic Byway.

It took about 200 million years to make the Cascades. Oregon is riding the collision of the North American continent with the Pacific plate subducting under it. As the Pacific plate ducks beneath, it melts under the tremendous pressure, and the hot basalt needs to find a way out. Thus, the older volcanic range of the western Cascades and the newer volcanoes of the eastern Cascades pushed up in two phases. U.S. 20 has just passed over, in eastern Oregon, the results of the basalt flowing up through cracks rather than creating volcanoes just as at Craters of the Moon. The authors of the *Roadside Geology of Oregon*, suggest that the dormant volcanoes on the west are not permanently so and may blow at any time like Mount St. Helens just north in the same range.

Back on 20 at Bend, the climb over the mountains really begins. The town of Sisters, about 20 miles past Bend, has retained some of its rustic flavor. But the traveler is warned that summer is high season and making reservations a week in advance may not be time enough. After Sisters, it is pine forest and winding roads that could easily make susceptible travelers car sick. Other snow-capped volcanoes come into view. The highway goes through Santiam Pass at 4817 feet.

Cascading (pun intended) down the western side of the Cascades with hairpin turns finally brings us to the Sweet Home Valley. The valley was first settled in 1851. The first community in this valley was named Buckhead after the name of the Buckland saloon on nearby Ames Creek. Another community a short distance from Buckhead was called Mossville. By the 1880's the two communities had expanded toward each other and the combined village was named Sweet Home. The City of Sweet Home was incorporated in 1893.

Past Sweet Home, 20 crosses the agriculturally productive Willamette River Valley. Here we find another example of the immigration and emigration across the continent in the family Schultheis saga from Bavaria. After a short stop in Missouri in 1836 and then Minnesota in 1854, they headed for Oregon's Willamette valley. The next generation homesteaded in Washington's Palouse River valley, a tributary of the Snake.

We pass through Lebanon and Albany to Corvallis. Corvallis strikes the traveler as a small university town and *is* the site of Oregon State University as well as the county seat for Benton County. The county was named after Thomas Hart Benton, the US senator who, with his colleague Lewis F. Linn, advocated the extension of US control into the Oregon country. Benton sent his son-in-law, Fremont, to "survey" this extension. (See chapter seven) The county was created out of an area originally inhabited by the Klickitat, who rented it from the Kalapooias for use as hunting grounds. All Indian claims to land within Benton County were ceded in the Treaty of Dayton in 1855.

It is now only a relatively short trip over the coastal range to Newport. The Coast Range is a slab of sea floor pushed up and mixed with mudstone and sandstone sediment as the Pacific plate ducked under the continent. Again, some winding roads are in store. But the end is worth the wait. Newport contains several gems at the end of the this long trail.

NEWPORT, LINCOLN COUNTY

population 45,277, 90% white, remainder Indian or Latino

U.S. 20 ends at U.S. 101 within view of the ocean. This traveler continued on nearly to the beach, turned left to Yaquina Bay State Park and light house. An exit leads down to the Historic Bayfront with fish processing plants on the ocean side and quaint buildings on the other. The Trident Sea Foods building has a picture of a whale on its outer wall. Newport, with Astoria, is one of Oregon's two major fishing ports, both ranking in the top twenty of fishing ports in the U.S. Its port averaged 105 million pounds of fish landed in 1997-2000. There are charters available for the different seasons of fishing: steelhead, sturgeon, crabbing, clamming, and salmon depending on the month. There are also whale watch tours when appropriate.

The history of Newport involves lumber shipping, tensions with Toledo several miles up the Achene River, several attempts at building harbors, and a failed railroad to Boise. Lumber from the saw mills in Toledo needed deeper water for the ships. At the same time, Newport needed jetties so that the passage over the bar at the entrance could handle larger ships going to California or Hawaii. Eventually the two port authorities joined forces but continued to have a hard time creating safe harbors. At one time, it took three separate votes for Newport to wrest the county seat from Toledo.

As lumber shipping decreased, commercial fishing and pleasure boating from Achene Harbor increased. A railroad was begun from Yaqluina Bay to Boise. It got to Corvallis and Albany and a bed laid to Hogg Summit in the Cascades before the company ran out of money. Then the automobile ended the need for passenger service over the coastal range and the track was torn up. Today, hundreds of pleasure boats rest at their docks around the bay. Their owners populate the surrounding hills, some during the summer, some all year.

The next stop to get the flavor of this ocean is the Oregon Coast Aquarium located across the Yaquina Bay bridge. A significant portion is in the open with venues for the Sea Otters, sea birds, Plovers as well as other attractions. There are touchpools for the children and one large octopus.

Just past the aquarium is the Oregon State University Hatfield Marine Science Center (http://hmsc.oregonstate.edu/visitor). This is also child friendly but much more science oriented. It is hands on science with a shocking exhibit of the invasion of native wildlife habitats by foreign aquatic species.

Another history of invasion is described in the Hatfield Marine Science Center: the destruction of the Siletz. The plaque states, "Contact with Euro-Americans in the 1700s was with European fur traders who sailed up the coast looking for beaver. With the arrival of Europeans comes new technology, trade goods and disease and erosion of the land and the people. In 1855, to make room for white settlers, the U.S. government creates the Coast (Siletz) Reservation. Indians are removed from their homelands and forced to move to 1.1 million acres of the reservation."

In 1875 the reservation was reduced to 225,000 acres

In 1892 it was broken into 80acre parcels which were sold to whites when Indians were not available for the "surplus."

In 1956 the U.S. Government determined that they are no longer Indians and terminated the tribe. After some decline the tribe coalesced and petitioned for tribal status.

In 1977 the government restored their tribal status. They maintain three thousand acres in Lincoln County.

Other Native Americans suffered under the white invasion. The Rogue River Indians in southern Oregon and northern California had enough in 1853 and began attacking white families. The army was sent and finally killed enough of the Indians to force the Flat Rock Treaty.

This ends the trail of history across six states. A rich history of people pushing westward and people being pushed out of the way. But I promised a sketch of some of the men who initiated the pushing in these states. On to the explorers.

CHAPTER SEVEN:
CROSSING THE EXPLORERS' TRAILS

Before we leave this voyage across half the continent, the contributions by some of the major characters need more recognition. This U.S. 20 corridor is a major crossroads in the explorations of the West rivaling the Santa Fé Trail in importance. Of course, it all began with the Lewis and Clark expedition clipping the boarders of Iowa and Nebraska. Before the company had returned to St. Louis in 1806, John Colter was permitted to drop out at the Mandan village on the Missouri and accompany two other men to the Yellowstone River to trap beaver.

Less than 40 years later, the editor of the *United States Magazine and Democratic Review*, which contained the reprints of John Charles Fremont's two expeditions, editorialized that no nation could be allowed to prevent "the fulfillment of our *manifest destiny* to overspread the continent allotted by Providence for the free development of our yearly multiplying millions."

Who were these men who opened up the West to emigration, mining and suppression of the Native American way of life? Their chronology from beaver trapping to Indian wars mirrors the taming of the West.

MANUEL LISA

Lewis and Clark returned to St. Louis in 1806, reporting a country rich in beaver, friendly Indians, and a transportation route up the Missouri River. This news generated a small stampede in 1807, as entrepreneurs prepared outfits to ascend the Missouri River. A trader named Manuel Lisa led the way.

Leading a party of 42 trappers and voyagers, Lisa and his brigade manhandled a keel boat up the Missouri and Yellowstone Rivers. Lisa constructed a fort where the Bighorn River flows into the Yellowstone. For the next year, Lisa directed trapping and trading operations from Fort Manuel before returning to St. Louis with a fortune in furs and new wisdom. He concluded that only large trading companies could operate efficiently and profitably. Soliciting a group of St. Louis merchants, Lisa formed the Missouri Fur Company in 1809, the first of the large American fur trading companies to work the upper Missouri

JOHN COLTER

On his way back from his trapping expedition, John Colter ran into Liza at his fort. Liza convinced Colter to return to Crow country to convince the Indians to trade at Fort Manuel. Some consider Colter the discoverer of the Yellowstone Park area. After years of research and conjecture, the conclusion must be reached that John Colter's route will never be known. He described geysers and hot springs that may have been in Yellowstone country and may have visited Jackson Hole on his 500-mile hike. Whatever this first white man's route was, he was in Wyoming (1807-08).

ANDREW HENRY

In 1810, Andrew Henry, a partner in Liza's company, led an expedition from Fort Manuel to the Three Forks of the Missouri River, the heart of Blackfoot and Gros Ventre territory. This formidable confederacy drove Henry's brigade out of this beaver-rich land into Pierre's Hole, Idaho. Then the trappers retreated to the Henry's Fork on the Snake River, where they established a fort. From Henry's Fort built at this spot, the rivers and streams of Jackson Hole were trapped for the first time in 1810-1811. In 1811, Henry disbanded the starving company, after a miserable winter at the first American post west of the Continental Divide. Three trappers, John Hoback, Edward Robinson, and Jacob Reznor headed east, crossing Teton Pass into Jackson Hole and exiting the valley via Togwotee Pass (Wind River Mountains). On the Missouri River, the veteran trappers met Wilson Price Hunt's brigade of Astorians bound for the Pacific Coast.

WILSON PRICE HUNT

Hunt was a St. Louis merchant at 21. In 1809, he met with John Jacob Astor concerning the latter's plan for a northwestern fur empire. Hunt became leader of the overland Astorians and was to take charge of the Columbia River post where the project would center. The land party left St. Louis late in 1810, wintering a few miles below the junction of the present states of Missouri, Kansas and

Nebraska. The group left to head up the Missouri River April 21, 1811, engaging in a "race" of sorts with Manuel Lisa for the last few hundred miles to the Arikara villages.

He bought horses from Lisa deciding was safer to travel cross country rather than on rivers lined with Indian danger. It is difficult to follow Hunt's route from maps and descriptions but it seems his party traveled up the Little Missouri into Wyoming's Thunder Basin, crossing the Powder River, the Big Horn Mountains and the Big Horn River and through the Wind River Range crossing the continental divide at Union Pass. At the Snake River (known then as the Mad River), Wyoming, they ran into difficulty before crossing the Tetons at Teton Pass. The Tetons were seen from a distance as obvious goals called Piolet Knobs, then Three Paps, Les Trois Tetons, and finally the Tetons.

Crossing into Idaho, they meet the Snake River (Idaho) and more problems (see the Idaho chapter). Starvation seemed to accompany the band forced to eat their moccasins, horses and dogs. They broke into three parties and finally reached Fort Astoria in January and February 1812.

ROBERT STUART

The War of 1812 had changed the situation and it was decided to dispatch a group of men, led by Robert Stuart, eastward, to inform Astor. Stuart left with six men on June 29, 1812. He went back to the Rocky Mountains much by the same way as Hunt had come, but in southern Idaho met an Indian who told them of a shorter route across the mountains than the one Hunt had followed. When he got to Jackson Hole he went down the Green River Valley and crossed the continental divide at South Pass.

To keep the trappers out of Oregon land, the British sent Peter Skene Ogden along the east side of the Cascades to assess the beaver population in 1820. Finding few, he decided the Americans would not come into the territory. But John Charles Fremont did just that on his 1843-44 expedition to California traveling south following Ogden's route. Ogden is best known for ransoming the 54 survivors of the Whitman Massacre (1847).

To find men for the first expedition of what would become the Rocky Mountain Fur Company, William Ashley and Andrew Henry ran this advertisement in the *St. Louis Gazette and Public Advertiser* in the winter of 1822: "Enterprising Young Men . . . to ascend the Missouri to its source, there to be employed for one, two, or three years." Such men as Jedediah Smith, Etienne Provost (after whom Provo Utah would be named), Jim Bridger, Thomas Fitzpatrick, and Hugh Glass (about whom the book *Lord Grizzly* was written) answered the call.

JEDEDIAH SMITH

Smith quickly proved himself and became the leader of subsequent parties from 1823-1830. Smith explored both the Rocky Mountains and the southwest. Over the course of his explorations he rediscovered the South Pass, went all the way to Arizona, across the Mojave desert to California, then up to Oregon and back across the Great Basin. On this foray, he was jailed by Mexican authorities in California for invading their territory and trapping beaver which were taken from him. Released, he headed for Oregon and was attacked by Indians and stripped of more pelts and horses. Trekking on to the Hudson's Bay Company post at Fort Vancouver, the factor (manager) there, John McLoughlin, sent a party to get his horses and skins back. Upon their return, he promised never to enter Oregon land again.

On one of his treks, he crossed the Snake River in Idaho, transected the Snake River Basin to the Salmon River all the way through Idaho to Montana and Clark's Fork. His route would have transected U.S. 20 near Arco.

On another route he crossed the Powder River, the Bighorn Mountains and river and went south to the Sweetwater River and South Pass obviously crossing U.S. 20 at least one point. On May 27, 1831, while en route to Santa Fé, Jedediah Smith was surrounded and killed by Comanche Indians at a water hole near the Cimarron River. His body was never found.

NATHANIEL WYETH

Unfortunate Nathaniel Wyeth, a New Englander, was making money cutting river ice when he fell under the spell of a promoter of Oregon colonization, a place neither man had seen. Wyeth put his savings into a trading company to buy furs and salmon. His band of tenderfoots joined William Sublette's company in 1832. Forced into eating the inner bark of balsam trees, the starving company stumbled into the rendezvous, according to one history, at the Green River, but more likely Pierre's Hole. There most of the company, including his brother, John, abandoned the adventure and headed back to St. Louis with Sublette.

Attempting to trap the western side of the Tetons, he found few beaver and continued to Walla Walla and down the Columbia to Vancouver. The ship that he expected to bring his supplies had sunk. He explored the Willamette Valley and then headed home to plan another expedition.

He returned with missionaries for Oregon, in 1834, and with more finances to supply Milton Sublette at the next rendezvous. Struggling into Wyoming, he reached Sublette's Fort at the junction of the North Platte and the Laramie River. On to the Sweetwater and then South Pass, he learned that Sublette had made a deal with Thomas Fitzpatrick to supply him at the Green River Rendezvous and would not receive Wyeth's $3,000 worth of goods. The revelry and deprivations of the rendezvous was a shock for the missionaries

Wyeth headed for the Bear River and Oregon. Meeting up with Capt. Bonneville (see below), the two men decided to place a fort at the junction of the Pontneuf and Snake Rivers. Wyeth called it Fort Hall. There the missionaries left Wyeth to follow Thomas McKay to the Willamette Valley. Wyeth followed to the Columbia River and attempted to trap beaver with little luck.

Wyeth's dreams of making a fortune ended with the dissolution of the Columbia River Fishing and Trading Company and his sale of Fort Hall to the Hudson Bay Company. He went back to cutting ice. The missionary settlement in the Willamette Valley turned out to be just as unsuccessful.

JIM BRIDGER

Silk hats and the diminishment of the beaver ended the fur trade. The last rendezvous was held in 1840. Mountain men became guides to military explorations and emigrants. Jim Bridger turned to a service career. He established Fort Bridger near the Oregon and California Trails and provided well-needed supplies for the wave of emigrants from 1842-1848. He guided Captain Howard Stanbury through what would become Bridger's Pass in 1850. This route shortened the Oregon Trail by 61 miles and would eventually be the route of the overland mail, the Union Pacific Railroad, and even Interstate 80.

Once Bridger canoed down the Bear River in Utah until he found a huge body of salt water. He thought he had reached the Pacific Ocean. In reality, Bridger had discovered the Great Salt Lake. In 1859, Bridger led Captain Raynold's surveying expedition to the Yellowstone area. For the next eight years he would guide and counsel military commanders in the opening campaigns of the war with the Sioux Indians.

THOMAS FITZPATRICK

Thomas Fitzpatrick also wore many hats in the opening of the west. Like Kit Carson, he accompanied Fremont on his second expedition and, in 1842, he led the very first missionary/emigrant group of Bidwell and Bartleson to California. This group was also the first to stop at newly erected Fort Bridger. In 1845, Fitzpatrick led Colonel Stephan Watts Kearney's trip to establish a military presence on the route to Oregon.

JOE WALKER

The only mountain man who could rival the greatness of Jedediah Smith was Joe Walker. For over half a century he roamed the west, trapping beaver, blazing trails, and leading expeditions. Perhaps Walker's greatest triumph was the trail he blazed to California in 1832 in the company of Capt. Benjamin Bonneville. Bonneville claimed he was on leave from the army to take up fur trapping, but many historians think he was an undercover agent for the US government--sent to spy on the Mexicans in California.

It is sure, however, that the route blazed by Bonneville and Walker was critically important because it turned out to be the only practical route to California. In future years, hundreds of thousands of pioneers would follow their footsteps to the promised land. Nearly a half-century later, the transcontinental railroad--seeking the best route west--would lay their tracks directly on top of Joe Walker's trail.

ZACHARY TAYLOR

Virginian Zachary Taylor's (1784-1850) life spans the history described in both volumes. Descendant of Pilgrim William Bruster and related to James Madison and Robert E. Lee, he grew up in Louisville, Kentucky on a large plantation. In 1808, he was commissioned a second lieutenant having little or no formal education and military training. He defended Fort Harrison from Tecumsah's attack in September 1812. He was part of an expedition near the old Tippecanoe site on the Wabash in which a group of rangers fell into an ambush. Reduced in rank, he was back in the army in 1819 to take a significant part in the Black Hawk War. He was promoted brigadier general after subduing Seminole Indians in Florida. He instigated the U.S. - Mexican War on the Rio Grande and led the victorious forces at the Battles of Palo Alto, Monterrey and Buena Vista. Riding on his fame, he ran for president in 1848. A large slave owner, he allowed western states to write constitutions as anti-slavery but died in office leaving the slavery question to Fillmore and the Compromise of 1850.

JOHN CHARLES FREMONT

Which brings us to the spying operations of John Charles Fremont, the *Pathfinder*, and Kit Carson. Fremont headed three expeditions west. During the first, 1842, he mapped most of the Overland Trail as far as South Pass and ascended the second highest peak in the Wind River Mountains, afterward called Fremont Peak. Fremont's reports, edited by his wife, the daughter of Sen. Thomas Heart Benton, stimulated the rush to Oregon. Sen. Benton was a strong advocate of western expansion.

In 1843, Fremont completed the survey of the Oregon Trail to the mouth of the Columbia River. He then traveled down the eastern side of the Cascades to California. Here he nearly perished trying to cross the Sierras. His group's tribulations, including having to eat their starving horses, mules and dogs, were prescient for the trials of the future Donner party. Nevertheless, his second report influenced Brigham Young to launch the Mormon trek to Utah and indirectly the Texas annexation as a state and the United States-Mexican War.

Fremont made his third expedition in 1845, further exploring both the Great Basin and the Pacific coast where he just happened to be when the Bear Flag Revolt broke out. When Monterey was occupied by American forces, in marched Fremont's band of mountain men. He served briefly as governor of California in 1847 while it was under military occupation. He resigned from service on March 15, 1848 after political problems with General Kearny. He was the first Republican candidate for President in 1854 losing to James Buchanan. Appointed to the command of the Department of the West at the start of the Civil War, Lincoln fired him for precipitously freeing the slaves. He was appointed territorial governor of Arizona from 1878 to 1881.

KIT CARSON

A young Kit Carson challenged a bully at the 1835 Green River rendezvous and in the subsequent duel tamed him by shooting him in the hand and arm. In 1842, while returning to Missouri to visit his family, Kit Carson happened to meet

Fremont, who soon hired him as a guide. Over the next several years, Carson helped guide Fremont to Oregon and California, and through much of the Central Rocky Mountains and the Great Basin. His service with Fremont, celebrated in Fremont's widely-read reports of his expeditions, quickly made Kit Carson a national hero, presented in popular fiction as a rugged mountain man capable of superhuman feats.

Before he met Fremont, Carson used Taos, New Mexico, as a base camp for repeated fur-trapping expeditions that often took him as far West as California. Later in the 1830's his trapping took him up the Rocky Mountains and throughout the West. For a time in the early 1840's, he was employed by William Bent as a hunter at Bent's Fort.

Carson would accompany Fremont on two more expeditions and, as a result of these military connections, fight in the Mexican War. He would continue to serve his country as an Indian agent for the Ute Indians in Taos from 1853-1861.

When the Civil War broke out, Carson eventually rose to the rank of Brigadier General. Beginning in 1863 Carson waged a brutal economic war against the Navajo, marching through the heart of their territory to destroy their crops, orchards and livestock. The Utes, Pueblos, Hopis and Zunis, who for centuries had been prey to Navajo raiders, took advantage of their traditional enemy's weakness by following the Americans onto the warpath. The Navajo were unable to defend themselves. In 1864 most surrendered to Carson, who forced nearly 8,000 Navajo men, women and children to take what came to be called the "Long Walk" of 300 miles from Arizona to Fort Sumner, New Mexico, where they remained in disease-ridden confinement until 1868.

After the Civil War, Carson moved to Colorado in the hope of expanding his ranching business. He died there in 1868, and the following year his remains were moved to a small cemetery near his old home in Taos.

THE NORTH BROTHERS

Few histories of the West include the story of Frank and Luther North and the Pawnee scouts. The boys were raised near Omaha, Nebraska in the 1840s where Frank learned some Pawnee language. In 1860, Frank was asked to translate for Indian agents at the Pawnee reservation. In 1864, he was asked to organize Pawnee scouts under General Curtis. Frank and the scouts played a leading role in the skirmishes with the same band of Sioux and Cheyenne involved in the Platte bridge battle where Caspar Collins was killed. The battles occurred near the new fort to be named Fort Reno. The three-pronged expedition to the Yellowstone River had left the North Platte and crossed the Niobrara, to the Powder River and the Big Horn Mountains.

In 1867, Frank was appointed Major of the Pawnee scouts and, with his brother, was part of expeditions around the North Platte, the Loupe and the Niobrara Rivers. They continued to clash with Indians in southern Nebraska. By 1871, Frank was stationed at Fort D.A. Russel in Wyoming near the present city of Cheyenne.

In 1874, Luther North accompanied Professor George Bird Grinnell (an author of a biography of the North brothers) and Gen. Custer into the Black Hills where gold was discovered. In 1876, the scouts were part of the roundup of Red Cloud near Chadron Creek and the escort to Ft. Robinson. Then they were off to attack Dull Knife's village near the Powder river. This was the last use of the scouts. The North brothers briefly owned a ranch with Cody on the Dismal River in the Sandhills.

CHIEF WASHAKIE OF THE SHOSHONE

This Native American holds a special place in the expansion into the West. He continued to be friends with the whites during his long life (1796-1900). When he sold the land that would become Thermopolis, he stipulated that the hot springs must benefit all. He continued a long cooperation with the U.S. government. His daughter married Jim Bridger. In a1868 Treaty, the Wind River Basin was designated as Shoshone land. When the government did nothing to stop whites from settling illegally or other Indian groups from attacking them, Washakie moved his entire tribe to Fort Bridger, where he camped out and refused to leave until the 1872 treaty was signed. The treaty established Fort Brown for the protection of the Shoshone, but in exchange they were forced to sell 600,000 fertile acres of Popo Agie River territory for a mere $25,000.

Washakie's forces fought with General Crook against the Lakota and Cheyenne in the Battle of the Rosebud during the summer of 1876. Although the confrontation was a stand off, Washakie has received credit for influencing Crook's decision not to pursue the allied Indian armies further. He advised Crook to, "Leave them alone for a few days. They cannot subsist their large numbers in the camp and will have to scatter out for meat and pasturage. They will begin to fight among themselves and some will sneak away to their agencies." When General Custer confronted the massed Indian armies only one week later, he met with total defeat. Washakie's strategy of divide and conquer finally won the war. When invited to meet with President Chester Arthur at Fort Washakie in 1883, the octogenarian chief invited the President to come to his tipi instead, which the president did.

THOMAS HART BENTON 1821-1851

The first senator for the new state of Missouri was an ardent supporter of westward expansion. Senator for a slave state, he brought his slaves to Washington D.C. But he vigorously opposed expansion of slavery west as a fiery opponent of Senator John C. Calhoun whose rhetoric served as the basis for session and Civil War which Calhoun did not live to see. He opposed the annexation of Texas in 1844 angering southerners including those in Missouri of which there were quite a few (see Last Negro in County is Dead by this author). Opposing his party, he pacified the intense debate over battling the British over Oregon Territory – "fifty-four forty or fight." He was defeated after serving 30 years by the Missouri supporters of slavery. Yet did prevent the division of California to be half slave and half free. Even after his death his presence convinced Missouri not to join the Southern Confederacy.

WOMEN

The role of women gets a short shrift in this history. We know a few by name such as Narcissi Whitman who followed her dream of missionary work. Men may have been the major part of the vanguard of emigration, but it was the women who kept up with them. I imagine the women pulling the Mormon handcarts across the Wyoming dessert as personifying the pioneer spirit. Some of them died in the snows of Wyoming.

When women left "civilized society" behind they found difficulty with the simplest tasks such as cooking without firewood, washing without water in any kind of weather encumbered by full skirts. The soddies leaked; the floors were hard-packed soil; and they lived with mice, bed bugs and snakes. The family bath served two or three persons and then was used to wash laundry. Not only cholera but also childhood diseases such as measles stalked their communities. An estimated 1700 grave sites lined the Platte River along the Overland Trail.

****

In retrospect, there is little doubt that the U.S. government "topographical expeditions" through the west were in preparation for expansion to the Pacific Ocean. Lewis and Clark did enter into British-claimed Oregon territory. From the Joint Occupancy Treaty of 1818 to 1846 when the British relinquished claim to Oregon lands, both countries tried to expand their operations.

Expeditions into the Great Basin and California were invasions of Mexican territory. President James Polk, first trying to buy the southwestern area claimed by Mexico, planned for war in 1845. Gen. Zachary Taylor sent troops into Mexican territory provoking the Mexicans to attack in 1846. The U.S. attacked in turn. In the end, Mexico lost most of the southwest and California. The same year, 1846, Oregon territory was recognized as belonging to the U.S. The war ended in 1848. The next year gold was discovered at Sutters Fort and the human stampede was on.

Picture Panel

Trolley, Rockford, Illinois

Basilica of St. Francis Xavier

The plow that won the West

Irma Hotel

Fort Boise, Parma Idaho

EPILOGUE

I do not wish to end our history on the sad note of the treatment of Native Americans that is documented along the way. By traveling this "blue highway," the full dimensions of the vastness and the diversity of the topography across these northern states can be thoroughly appreciated. From the glacier-sculpted Midwest to the flatlands of Iowa and Nebraska, from the high desert of Wyoming to the Rockies, from the volcanic deposits of Idaho to the tree-covered Cascades and from the valley of the Willamette to the ocean fisheries, this land is trapper country, emigrant trails, railroad right of ways, cattle and cowboy land, soldier campgrounds and Indian villages. One can feel the hopes and agonies of those who passed through, those who stopped and stayed, and those who died trying to stem the flood of emigrants.

Now this wave of pioneers can only be felt in replicas of their life in dugouts and forts, in soddies and cabins. Sadly the population of many of these areas is diminishing as the mechanization of farming and the pull of the cities gives less promise to the next generation. The plaque in Worland describes the dream: "... drawing pioneer men and women possessing an indomitable spiritual force dreaming that Big Horn River water would create a new way of life here in the desert."

Water is the unifying factor in this trek. Water from the Rockies draining into the Missouri and Mississippi or into the Snake and Columbia. Water from the Cascades. Ancient water from the great aquifers. Water turned into cattle feed, potatoes, and soy beans. Much of this region depends on snow rather than rain for its irrigation water. One can only wonder what global warming will do to these sources of life-giving water.

A recent article in the New York Times, "A Farmer Fears His Way of Life Has Dwindled Down to a Final Generation," accurately describes the human conditions in the West. From Rockford to the Oregon coast, the populations in counties alone the U.S. 20 corridor are shrinking (See Table 2). Only where tourism flourishes, such as Galena, Bend or Newport, is the population increasing. Absentee owners hirer tenants to push their machines over the land in larger and large plots. Boarded up businesses in the small towns, abandoned by the railroads and the bus lines, line main streets. Former industries that hired the local farmers or their wives have shut their doors.

The age of the yeoman farmer/rancher is drawing to a close just as the ages of the Native Americans, the trappers and the explorers ended. The only constant is the land itself: the great rivers, the majestic mountains, high deserts or sand hills and hot springs. This geologic history is just as exciting to the traveler as the brief history of western expansion. Why whiz by on the interstate highways when the U.S. 20 corridor across the west is so attractive?

One answer is the opportunity to taste the ambience of food establishments in the absence of the fast food venues that seem to sprout at every major intersection along the interstates. Breakfast and information was served at a corner café by a young woman of German extraction from German, a small community south of Freeport. Irish dancers were enjoyed at an Irish pub in Galena. Conversation with local farmers occurred at the Dyersville Family Restaurant. The Princes Sweet Shop in Iowa Falls offered fond childhood memories. The Old Johnson Hotel Café in Plainview brought back more memories. In Valentine, the Bunkhouse Bar and Restaurant collected a wide range of local patrons as did a corner restaurant in Grey Bull and the Mine Company (restaurant) in Cody. Great conversations were held at the Pickle Place in Arco and the corner drive-in at Burns. Color and conversations that are hard to find along the interstates.

The Indian Wars along this corridor have been integrated into each state's history. The tidal wave across the continent, dredging out the Native Americans, would appear inevitable, Once the ethnic cleansing was over its effects were excused in wild west shows, books and film. Nevertheless, as the extent of the destruction comes forward, appreciation of the arrogance of the white man (the spider, *veho,* as the Cheyenne called him) brings little comfort to the surviving Red Man.

But that is only one aspect of frontier violence. Another is the near extinction of animal species such as the buffalo, bears, wolves, sea otters mostly for human vanity. But the most egregious is the violence of one white human on another white which should not be ignored in these travels.

Professor Richard Maxwell Brown calls the violence scattered throughout the West "the Western Civil War of Incorporation." It was a class war posting the wealthy ranchers or mine owners against the poorer: the Hispanoes of the Southwest (his designation), the settlers, small ranchers and miners. The ranchers used vigilante groups and gunfighters such as Wild Bill Hickok and Wyatt Earp as their enforcers. A recent article by Allen Barra in the *New York Times* (Oct. 26, 2006 pA27) confirms the story that the Gunfight at the OK Corral actually involved surrogates for the large ranchers against the "small ranchers who benefitted from the cowboys' illegal trafficking" in Mexican cattle.

"Stewart's Stranglers" terrorized Montana in the 1850s with the moral support of a young Teddy Roosevelt. The Regulators tried the same methods of murder and intimidation in Wyoming during the 1890s.

Prof. Brown asks, "Is the West mainly responsible for the American heritage of pervasive violence?" His answer is equivocal. During this period, English common law, which required that one retreat from aggression as far as possible, was turned around. No one could "back down." Garry Cooper in *High Noon* for example. State after state allowed "carrying" of firearms. Thus, a mythology of the gunfighter was created in novel and film and then television. Prof. Brown uses John Wayne as the primary icon. But he counts many more Indians killed in white perpetrated massacres than the opposite and many more ranchers, settlers and miners killed by whites rather than by Indians (Table 3).

On the other hand, one can argue that some violence was necessary to conquer the land "from sea to shining sea." In reality, the land could not be conquered only modified until the next drought, blizzard, fire or volcanic eruption. The course of nature will have its way with the land. No human modification is permanent from a geologic perspective. Traveling this U.S. 20 corridor allows a greater view of and appreciation of geologic history.

END

TABLE 1 GEOLOGIC HISTORY TO THE PRESENT
(shortened and annotated)

Precambrian (4,500 to 543 mya)*

Hadean (4500 to 3800 mya)	solar system forming
Archaean (3800 to 2500 mya)	appearance of bacteria
Proterozoic (2500 to 543 mya)	eukaryotic cells
Vendian (650 to 543 mya)	primitive animals

Phanerozoic (543 mya to today)

Paleozoic Era (543 to 248 mya) animals expand, diversify

Cambrian (543 to 490 mya)	trilobites common
Ordovician (490 to 443 mya)	bony fish
Silurian (443 to 417 mya)	life on land, early plants, spiders
Devonian (417 to 354 mya)	terrestrial vertebrates, larger plants, wingless insects
Carboniferous (354 to 2290 mya)	coal formed, Appalachian Mts. pushed up
Permian (290 to 248 mya)	mass extinction of sea and some land life, Pangea formed

Mesozoic Era (248 to 65 mya)
Triassic (248 to 206 mya)   dinosaurs
Jurassic (206 to 144 mya)   larger dinosaurs
Cretaceous (144 to 65 mya)   Dinosaurs disappear except
                                   birds, mammals appear

Cenozoic Era (65 mya to today)
Tertiary (65 to 1.8 mya)
    Paleocene (65 to 54.8 mya)
    Eocene 54.8 to 33.7 mya)   Green River Formation in
                                              Wyoming shows evidence
                                              of a warmer, wetter
                                              climate
    Oligocene (33.7 to 23.8 mya)
    Miocene (23.8 to 5.3 mya)
    Pliocene (5.3 to 1.8 mya)
Quaternary (1.8 mya to today) humanoids appear
    Pleistocene (1.8 mya to 10,000   mammoths, saber tooths,
    years ago)   recent ice ages
    Holocene (10,000 years ago to   dispersal of humans over
    today)   the globe

*million years ago
Data from Geological Society of America, <www.ucmp.berkeley.edu/help/autimeform.html>

TABLE 2 Population changes

COUNTY	POP/MI^2	TOWN ON 20	%POP +/-*
Winnebago, IL	542	Rockford	+3.7
Stephenson, IL	86	Freeport	-2.0
Jo Daviess, IL	37	Galena	+4.2
Dubuque, IO	147	Dubuque	+2.8
Webster, IO	56	Fort Dodge	-3.1
Woodbury, IO	873	Sioux City	-1.2
Pierce, NE	14	Plainview	-3.3
Antelope, NE	8.7	Royal	-6.0
Holt, NE	48	O'Neill	-6.6
Cherry, NE	1.0	Valentine	-0.8
Dawes, NE	24	Crawford	-4.7
Natrona, WY	12	Casper	+4.9
Converse, WY	2.8	Douglas	+5.9
Hot Springs, WY	2.0	Thermopolis	-7.1
Park, WY	4	Cody	+2.2**
Fremont, ID	6	St Anthony	+3.6
Madison, ID	58	Rexburg	+12.8
Bonneville, ID	44	Idaho Falls	+8.6**
Butte, ID	1.3	Arco	-3.1
Blaine, ID	5.0	Carey	+11.4
Camas, ID	1.0	Farifield	+2.2**
Elmore, ID	3.0	Mountain Home	-1.7
Ada, ID	285	Boise	+14.6

Payette, ID	50	Payette	+7.9
Mallheur, OR	3.0	Ontario	-0.9
Harney, OR	1.0	Burns	-9.3
Linn, OR	19	Sweet Home	+4.2**
Deschutes, OR	18	Bend	+22.5
Benton, OR	116	Corvallis	+0.6
Lincoln, OR	45	Newport	+3.4

* % change in population 2000-2005, **2000-2004

Table 3 MASSACRES, shoot-outs and ambushes not included

Indian on white: Whitman, Washington (1847), Ward (1854), Otter (1860) both in Idaho, Apache (1885) Arizona and New Mexico. 109 total deaths

White on white: Mountain Meadows by Mormons (1857). 130 total deaths

White on Indian: Bear River, Idaho (1863), Sand Creek (1864), Marias River (1870). Washita River (1868), Wounded Knee (1890). More than 700 total deaths

TABLE 4 Dates of Incorporation of Representative Towns and a Brief Chronology

Incorporated on
Illinois

- ❖ Rockford 1834
- ❖ Freeport 1827
- ❖ Lina 1834
- ❖ Galena 1827

Iowa

- ❖ Dyersville 1837
- ❖ Fort Dodge 1850

Nebraska

- ❖ Royal 1868
- ❖ O'Neal 1873
- ❖ Valentine 1882
- ❖ Chadron 1884
- ❖ Crawford 1886

Wyoming

- ❖ Casper 1888
- ❖ Shoshoni 1905
- ❖ Worland 1906
- ❖ Cody 1902

Oregon
- ❖ Burns 1889
- ❖ Bend 1905
- ❖ Newport 1882

Chronology Related to this Book

Lewis and Clark, 1805-06
Missouri Fur Company John Colter, 1807
Henry's company at Jackson Hole, 1811
Wilson Price Hunt Arrives at Astoria, 1812
Robert Stuart stumbles into South Pass, 1812
Rocky Mountain Fur Co., 1822
Bonneville's trek to California, 1832
Fort Bridger, 1842
Fremont's expeditions, 1842, 1843, 1845
Brittan gives up rights to Oregon, 1846
Mexican War, 1846-1848
Gold in California, 1849
North Platte Bridge Battle, 1865
Transcontinental railroad completed, 1868
Gold in the Black Hills, 1874
Fort Robinson internment, 1878-79
Wounded Knee, 1890

SOURCES

Research has changed from visits to the library and calls to authorities to hours on the World Wide Web. But with this revolution in information comes a caveat that every investigator must respect. Do not believe what your read. Check the facts.

In checking my facts, I used the newspaper reporter's dictum of at least two if not three sources. Of course Wickipedia speeds up the research but must be supported by other sources. For example the Idaho National Laboratory now has a facebook site.

I am indebted to John McPhee's two part series in *The New Yorker* (October 3 & 10, 2005) "Coal Train" for the description of that section.

McPhee's *Rising from the Plains* is a must read for anyone interested in Wyoming geology and history

I have relied heavily on *The Last Prairie, a Sandhills Journal* by Stephen R. Jones for the section about the Sandhills.

The Mountain Press Roadside series: *History of Idaho* by Betty B. Derig, ... *of Oregon* by Bill Gulick, ... *of Wyoming* by Candy Moulton; *Geology of Oregon* by Davi Alt and Donald Hyndman, and ... *of Wyoming* by Darwin Spearing and David Lageson the *Encyclopedia of Indian Wars*, Gregory F. Michno, ed contained useful gems of history

I found the *Oxford History of the American West* presented an excellent general picture of western expansion as well as fine vignettes.

The story of the *Orphan Trains* (by Annette Fry, 1994) is also available at <www.orphantrainriders.com>

The story of the North brothers can be found in *Two Great Scouts and their Pawnee Battalion* by George Bird Grinnell 1928 reprinted 1973

The Tide of Empire America's March to the Pacific by Michael Golay

Eyewitness to the American West, David Colbert, ed.

Pioneer Women, by Linda Peavy and Ursula Smith

<www.gorockford.com>
<www.andersongardens.org>
<www.tinkercottage.com>
<www.galina.org>
<www.desotohouse.com>
<www.rivermuseum.com>
<www.nationalfarmtoymuseum.com>
< www.fodmoviesite.com>
<www.iafalla.com/historic/Princess html>
<www.fortmuseum.com>
<www.furtrade.org>
<www.aquarium.org>